7517

"Brothers & Sisters, We Have a Problem"

"Brothers & Sisters, We Have a Problem"

Nicky Cruz

DOVE Christian Books

P.O. Box 36-0122 • Melbourne, FL 32936 • (407) 242-8290

Cover design, editorial work and typography by
Publications Technologies, Eau Gallie, Florida

Printed in the United States of America

DOVE Christian Books

P.O. Box 36-0122 • Melbourne, FL 32936 • (407) 242-8290

Preface

Being in the ministry for 26 years has positioned me to be vulnerable to the corrupting forces I discuss in this book.

I have seen it all. I believe we have choices to make today.

We can shrug off the seriousness of the corruption in our midst or we can choose to follow God's path. I cannot do anything but go God's way. That doesn't mean I am perfect or have never sinned before God. I have. And I still do. But I have come to terms with the direction I want to go. It is not always easy. There are painful consequences. Choosing God's path is not always glamorous. At times, it calls for sacrifices.

As I travel around the world, I have observed the condition of God's people today. I have seen changes in the Church and in Christian organizations. I have watched the rise of the Charismatic movement. I was there at the birth of the prosperity message. I have been a part of Christian TV and the Christian music industry. I've watched the evangelism message change. I have seen the growing threat of what I call Christian humanism. And I have been quiet too long. I can no longer contain the pressure of the Holy Spirit on my broken heart. My spirit aches. My eyes are filled with tears.

My desire is to share some of my experiences and help us recognize the way to victory. We are a mighty army. We are destined to conquer! We will rise to the challenge set before us. It may appear that we have been knocked down. But we are not out! We Christians are not to walk with our tails between our legs. We are to rise in glory and bounce back to make a powerful difference in the world! We must not be intimidated or discouraged—just strong and courageous, knowing the battle is ours!

God promises that despite the mistakes, pain, suffering and persecution, the victory is ours in Christ our Lord. Brothers and sisters, we will win! Praise His holy name!

Dedicated to my board of directors and their spouses: Dr. Jim and Joyce Caldwell, Mrs. Catherine McCormick, Jim and Jean Vick, Leon and Ruth Cairns, Gary and Marilyn Deaton, Chaplain Russell and Mary Skipper, the Rev. Fred and Jetta Smolchuk, John and Helen Taylor, Dr. John and Ginny Whitmire, and Dick and Gayle Withnell. Thanks.

Acknowledgments: For all the long months devoted to this book, thanks to my wife, Gloria, my pastor, Don Steiger, to Mrs. James (Mary) Irwin, and to my staff—particularly John Arana. Thanks to the folks at **Publications Technologies,** including the Lord's best copy editor, Jane Boyd. My gratitude also to Ray and Joyce Colenbaugh, Willa Kerby, Julie Frahm, Jann Zermeño, the Jerry Watson family, and the staff at **HIS Marketing.** And a special thanks to **DOVE Christian Books,** particularly my editor and publisher, Rob Kerby, who put in such long hours birthing this call to arms to God's people.

Brothers and sisters, we have a problem!

As I watch the young pastor, I am gripped with memory. He is articulate. His message, delivered in a drawl, is "Wake up, corrupted Church!"

His text is — more or less — from the Epistle of James: "Brothers and sisters," he says, "there's a heathen America out there that needs YOU to get out of your comfortable pews! It's dying! It's settling for fake christs! It's falling for witchcraft and astrology! *You* can do something about it! Take the joy of Jesus to the hungry, the homeless, the angry! *Wake up!* You have the answers. Share them! Put your faith to work!"

The young pastor excitedly begins to quote the late Keith Green:

"Do you see? Do you see all the people sinking down?
"Don't you care?
   "Don't you care? Are you going to let them drown?
"How can you be so dead —
   "When you've been so well fed?
"Jesus rose from the grave —
   "And you ... you can't even get out of bed!"

I want to jump to my feet and shout "Yes!" But remaining in my seat, I tremble with emotion. My turn will come soon enough.

I understand this young man's joy. I remember. Once, too, I was consumed with a youthful single-mindedness to win the world for Jesus all by myself. I couldn't do *anything* but preach Jesus. I was filled with the thrill of my newfound salvation. I had a wild urgency to get out there and rescue all my murdering buddies still hurting and dying in Brooklyn's concrete jungle.

But tonight, I am also filled with the pastor's anguish. His words are falling on deaf ears—and he knows it. This beautiful church sanctuary is a morgue. The people stare deadly at their earnest young man. You can see they want to hear something else. They want me to get up—me, the visiting superstar. They want me to talk about gangs and New York street fighting and things that happened three decades ago.

They want exciting stories. Milk for baby Christians—not meat for the mature believers they are...or *could be* if they would just stretch out their spiritual arms and put their faith back to work.

I know his impatience. Only the Holy Spirit can unlock these hearts. Only through fervent prayer. Tonight, the anointing isn't on this urgent young pastor, despite his enthusiasm and excitement. The folks are uncomfortable in the guilt he's laid upon them. They're making excuses there in their pews — *excuses* :

- *That only a few are called to evangelism. That evangelism is a spiritual gift of some sort and if you haven't got it, well, then you haven't got it.*

- *That the message of anything but prosperity, prosperity, prosperity is too negative to consider. God wants to bless us with His great riches ... and that's all that is really important!*

Excuses:

- *That those not called to spread the Gospel should stay home and send money to those who go.*

- *That TV evangelism is a shameful activity. Several of our most visible "televangelists" have been publicly humiliated — thus the rest are money-hungry, sex-happy hypocrites, too.*

Excuses:

- *That evangelism — particularly the tract-passing kind — was for the 1970s. It intrudes on people's personal space.*

- *That witnessing is offensive to people who share different belief systems. After all, who are you or I to tell a Mormon that Joseph Smith was a false prophet, possibly deceived by an angel of light straight from hell? Where do you or I get off declaring that Buddha or Christian Science founder Mary Baker Eddy or Indian mystic Krishna fell for the same lie that the serpent pulled on Eve—that we each can be wise as God?*

I pray that only a few in tonight's crowded sanctuary are excusing themselves with this terrible lie:

- *That here are many roads to truth and contrary to the Christian message, mankind is NOT made up of sinners in need of eternal salvation — nor is Jesus the ONLY way to eternal life and / or cosmic enlightenment. Such a view is downright closed-minded and probably a bigoted violation of someone's rights!*

Brothers and sisters, our Church is being lulled into surrender with such lies. Satan has begun his final assault and has caught the Church dazed, unprepared and disarmed.

"So, what?" you might say, "It's nothing new." Well, from its earliest days, as the Good News spread from Jerusalem throughout the known world, the corruption was underway. In Acts 20, Paul warned the elders of the church of Ephesus:

"I know full well that after I leave you, false teachers, like vicious wolves, will appear among you, not sparing the flock. Some of you yourselves will distort the truth in order to draw a following. Watch out! I have never been hungry for money or fine clothing — you know that these hands of mine worked to pay my own way and even to supply the needs of those who were with me." (Acts 20:29-31) [Unless otherwise noted, all scriptures quoted are from Kenneth Taylor's superb paraphrase of the ancient texts, *The Living Bible* © 1972 Tyndale House, Wheaton, Illinois]

The Epistles go on to tell how many in the brotherhood were quickly corrupted away from the Gospel. Paul fought the false teachers and profiteers throughout his letters. James and John in their letters are quite scathing on the subject of false or lazy teachers.

But the assault has continued with ever-increasing intensity. And in these final days of the Church on Earth, I believe the last big attack is mounting. **Why?** The Bible says the people of God should have *one* major mission and it is to go unto all the world and preach the Gospel to everyone.

Satan is determined to halt that. He hates God's one creation "in His own image" — man. He is determined to destroy and subvert and corrupt man up until the very last moments before being exiled for eternity into the pit. Satan has a number of resources — hatred, false accusation, confusion, greed, pride, selfish anger, to name a few — and he's unleashing everything now in this final assault. One example: the insidious lies of the ungodly supernatural. I'll have to tell you that I felt like weeping when some time back it was revealed the First Lady of the United States was heavily into astrology.

Folks, any supernatural not coming from God is absolutely forbidden to us! When Israel's King Saul went to a witch, his kingdom was immediately removed from him! He *died* in the next hours! But here is Mrs. Nancy Reagan insisting that President Reagan's daily schedule be plotted according to Mars rising and Pluto descending — or whatever.

This came on the heels of a noted actress sharing with us all in a best-selling book and top-rated made-for-TV movie that reincarnation is real and the occult is great fun!

No! And at the same time, terrible scandals are rocking the very foundations of the American Church. We've all wept in shame as some of our best-known spokesmen — caught in terrible sin — have refused to submit themselves to the very authorities with which they chose to align their ministries.

As a result, the cash flow to many effective outreaches has slowed to a trickle. And as the pagan news media gawks, civil war has erupted — Christian versus Christian — in what secular broadcasters and columnists jokingly call the "Holy Wars." We've all hidden our faces as our top leaders' dirty laundry — as well as the terrible, divided state of our brotherhood — is paraded on the evening news.

For example, on a special edition of the *McNeil Lehrer News Hour* on public television, Christian spokesmen got sidetracked quickly from discussing Pat Robertson's political future. Instead, they got into a baffling-to-the-outsider theological debate on biblical inerrancy and *charismata* — while the grinning secular hosts stood back and watched the fur fly.

Brothers and sisters, we are a house dangerously divided — and increasingly victimized by gossip-mongers in whose best interest it is to make us look like idiots! Furthermore, while we scratch each others' eyes out, our true enemy is leading an unprecedented attack — knowing that if we were paying any attention to him, we would drive him back in defeat.

Folks, it's time we regarded witchcraft and the occult from God's viewpoint. He is a jealous God. Constantly, He chooses in His sovereign power to wield majestic, miraculous intervention in each of our lives.

It's called answered prayer.

But when we seek or accept such power from any source other than our Creator, we break His unbendable laws, repeated throughout the Old and New Testaments. How specific are these divine rules? Consider Deuteronomy 18:9-10:

> *"When you arrive in the Promised Land you must be very careful lest you be corrupted by the horrible customs of the nations now living there. For example ... [no one] may practice black magic, or call on the evil spirits for aid, or be a fortune teller ...."*

As I write this, 28,000 witches have been fasting and praying for many months to their dark, false god for the disgrace and fall of the world's evangelists. How do I know this? I've been told by the witches themselves!

Should we shudder in fear of them? NO! No weapon they can devise against God's obedient children can prosper! Nothing they do can touch believers living in the Father's will. But they can do such damage to the unprotected! Just look at the cliff they're leading America over!

And what about those believers in rebellion — and out of God's will? What about those refusing to obey the Great Commission to evangelize their households, their neighborhoods, their schools, their workplaces, their cities, their states, their nations and their world?

What about those Christians flaunting immorality and refusing to obey authorities? What about believers who close their eyes to the spiritual storm around them and continue to seek after money, prosperity and material gain instead of things of God?

Don't ever forget what the Father allowed to happen to the Israelites. Look at His promise in I Samuel 12:20-22:

"...make sure now that you worship the Lord with true enthusiasm, and that you don't turn your back on him in any way. Other gods can't help you. The Lord will not abandon his chosen people, for that would dishonor his great name. He made you a special nation for himself—just because he wanted to!"

Then, move back up the chapter to verse 15 and take very seriously just one of the many warnings scattered throughout the Bible:

"If you rebel against the Lord's commandments and refuse to listen to him, then his hand will be as heavy upon you as it was upon your ancestors."

That's serious stuff. **We dare not ignore it.**

For centuries our wonderful Christian brotherhood has been splintered into ineffective little pockets of quarreling nit-pickers determined to fuss among themselves rather than unite and spread the Gospel. Our failure today is increasingly heartbreaking. While we fuss and back-stab, Lucifer's forces advance on every front—unopposed by the spiritual prayer warriors he so desperately fears! So, what keeps God's kingdom on Earth from repenting and charging into battle "in one accord?"

Just invite clergy and laity of the Greek Orthodox, Southern Baptist, Assemblies of God, United Church of Christ (Congregationalist), United Pentecostal Church, the Church of Christ/ Disciples of Christ/Christian Church movement, various synods of the Lutherans, the Presbyterians, the Seventh-Day Adventists, and Roman Catholic churches into one room and ask them to come up with a plan for world evangelism.

I pick on these since it's silly for me to pretend that God's work isn't being done by each of them — in creative and effective ways. But it's absurd for me to believe that such a meeting would even get under way before certain members would stomp out — *infuriated to be in the same room with the others!*

For those who remained, plans for outreach would be certain to get bogged down when the discussion reached the question of:

"What do we tell the lost they must *do* to be saved?"

The diabolical subversion has been effective. Many Christians hate their brothers. And now the results present us with a challenge:

• Leaders of our newest Christian generation have been raised in schools devoid of God and in front of TVs devoid of morality and filled with glorification of the occult. Dependence on our great, almighty God — daily dependence to the point of taking *everything* before Him — is ridiculed at school and on TV *and is barely taught in the home or in church.*

• This generation — *we, yes, you and I* — have heard such a steady stream of diabolical humanism until few can even recognize its lies, such as that each of us is the highest authority of what is right or wrong ... or that we can be anything we want to be if we will only believe in ourselves enough ... or that Christian fundamentalism is a threatening fanaticism that must be feared.

Yes, tonight, I am filled with this young pastor's frustration. The congregation stares back at him, baby boomers raised in a society that denies its Christian roots — sitting with their proud parents and their own rosy-cheeked kids. There is no denying this crowd is made up of good people seeking to be led of the Holy Spirit and to walk the walk. But the message in their human hearts has been so corrupted.

I see white-haired survivors of the Great Depression so scared that a thief will break in and take their *things* ... good Christians, yet so in bondage to possessions — and living in such fear that a new crash will leave them destitute again.

Don't they know our Lord's promises that we will never have to beg? That if we trust and do not fear, we will have our every need provided? That He does not lead us into the wilderness to die!

I see goal-oriented, middle-aged executives ... I see young, upwardly mobile professionals ... I see socially conscious kids in designer clothes and $100 tennis shoes. I yearn to see those youngsters taught by their parents to seek out the lost and the hurting and to give them Jesus. Don't moms and dads realize that by law Christian kids are now the only ones who can proclaim Jesus in America's public schools?

Their testimony is protected by the same freedom of expression that protects the pornographers. Only principals, parents, teachers and counselors are bound to silence on the school grounds. Yet, even that right is under attack now, too. So, kids, it may be now or never! How important is it to you that your buddies spend eternity in heaven with you?

I hurt as I stare out at this crowd. I know that in these career-oriented families, standing up for Jesus in public is considered ... well, "ineffective, given the big picture." The unstated strategy becomes to lay low. Keep the salvation message to yourself. Don't bring embarrassment on yourself. *Embarrassment!?*

What's happened? American Christians today don't fear being thrown to the lions or being exiled to the gulag. They fear social *embarrassment!* The Great Commission to them has become:

"Go ye unto all the world and act just like they do and hope they're so impressed you're not a fuddy-duddy that they'll bring up the subject of Jesus so you never have to. If they do, keep it light. Don't hassle anybody. Buy them a drink! You've got an image, a career and a future to think of. Keep the big picture in mind."

As this excited, earnest young pastor preaches on, I realize my knuckles are white, my fist gripped in anger.

I shake, in a cold sweat — as if I have awakened in a nightmare. I feel as if I should forget about speaking tonight. I should urge this young man to preach on! *But I don't.* I stand as he introduces me. I tremble with emotion. But I feel a hesitancy. "Listen to your fine young man of God!" I want to shout. But it's as if the Holy Spirit is cautioning me to more slowly. I should go ahead and tell a story.

That's what they came wanting to hear.

A story, not a sermon.

Should I tell them the same old stuff about being an angry, murderous kid leading a street gang of 200 — and how David Wilkerson led me to Jesus when I suddenly didn't have it in me to steal the offering he'd had me and my jitterbugging buddies collect from the crowd?

The story is so old. God still uses it in amazing ways to win the lost in surprising places. Poland. Miami. England. Detroit. Mexico. *But here?*

I pray silently that the Holy Spirit will touch these folks and they will somehow hear my heart since I know I must not *preach* condemnation and guilt to them — as I certainly would if I were to try to minister only in my own strength and wisdom ... and anger.

Suddenly, the Lord stirs in my heart a different story to tell them.

Yes! I'll tell them of my recent travels to West Germany and Brazil where witchcraft is sweeping through like a mighty flood. I'll tell of the confrontation I had with satanic leaders in Holland, where five of the high priests challenged me to a debate. Instead, the power of the Lord swept through our meeting hall and two of the satanist leaders fell to their knees in awe of almighty God and gave their lives to Jesus while their friends screeched and howled and fled!

I'll talk about an evening in the Third World when native witch doctors converged on our enormous crusade in the National Stadium and attempted to call down the evil of demon spirits to destroy our service — and how the majesty and might of our true Creator rippled through the place, throwing the evil sorcerers to the ground as the crowd rose to its feet, stunned at the unquestionable demonstration of He who is mightier than the prince of darkness.

Tears come to my eyes as I see the dead congregation come to life. I can tell they love stories of miracles. O Lord, I whisper, touch their selfish hearts. I can see that they want to be entertained now. They expect me to form a prayer line and spend the next half hour touching their heads and letting the power of the Lord jolt them to the floor "slain in the spirit."

No, the Holy Spirit tells me. Not this time. This crowd is not like the unbelievers of whom Jesus spoke in John 4:48, "Won't any of you believe in me unless I do more and more miracles?" No, this bunch has seen miracles and wonders. *They believe.* They don't need a Christian magic act. They need to be eating spiritual meat. I pray that they will see that they can ... no, *must* ... change the world. That's our job! But, I must be careful. I must not heap more guilt on these do-nothing, bless-me-bless-me Christians.

I *want* to talk to them about holiness. About yearning for the mind of Christ. About putting our eyes on Jesus and discovering that we don't have to worry about anything else — including evangelism and fighting Satan! If we are moving in the Father's will, He will guide us in His plan for all of this stuff! Hebrews 6:1-2 keeps coming to mind:

> *"Let us stop going over the same old grown again and again, always teaching those first lessons about Christ. Let us go on instead to other things and become mature in our understanding, as strong Christians ought to be. Surely we don't need to speak further about the foolishness of trying to be saved by being good or about the necessity of faith in God ... The Lord willing, we will go on now to other things."*

But how do I accomplish this?

Should I be content with manipulating them into action? Tricking them? For example, on a purely selfish level, evangelism is very self-fulfilling. So, do I appeal to their self-centered obsession with *feeling good* about themselves? Shall I motivate them by telling of the personal excitement they will feel as they watch a friend accept Jesus and the incredible joy and peace that floods your soul when you lead somebody to the Lord? No, that won't accomplish the Father's purpose.

Instead I tell of another enormous crusade. This time, Satan's evil agent was an old gang member rival from my youth. He still blamed me for terrible knife scars I'd put on his face.

I tell how he had stalked me from city to city as I led crusades in the 1960s. I tell how his one reason to live became simply to kill me. How I preached Jesus to him one evening as he hid in an immense crowd.

How he found the Lord that night.

How he answered the altar call.

How, as he hugged me, I felt the gun under his coat — the pistol he had brought with the intent of gunning me down in front of thousands.

Does tonight's crowd understand? That God protects us from even the most enormous evil when we are obedient? That there is such great joy in transforming your most violent enemies into God-praising brothers in Christ — through the power of the Holy Spirit?

At home, I know that my beautiful wife, Gloria, is interceding on her knees on my behalf — and for this sleepy congregation and others like it around the world. She's praying that the Lord will touch their lives. That they will listen to His urging to get about their Father's business.

And I try to relax in the peaceful joy of knowing God is in control.

This lazy bunch is really not my problem.

My problem is being obedient as the Lord shows me how to be His servant as He sets about to call them into war.

Spiritual war.

A war in which we are guaranteed victory — if we will just put on our armor, listen to our Commander's voice, and discipline ourselves into obeying when we'd rather retreat in the face of the enemy.

You see, the darkness can never win the war.

Just an occasional battle.

As I speak, I tell of my mother, who during my childhood was a voodoo priestess in my native Puerto Rico. I tell of her terrible, cutting words when I was eight years old:

"Nicky, I hate you."

Mere words.

They rang in my ears, taunting me, tormenting me for years until I gave my heart to Jesus one night. A man I'd sworn to kill refused to stop loving me. I cursed him, closed my mind to his words, and slammed his smiling, forgiving face into a wall.

David Wilkerson's love changed me forever. Without it, I would never have believed Jesus' love. If he'd preached condemnation to me, I might have really killed him — just to show him who was boss: "So, I'm going to hell, Preacher? Guess what? I *know* that! Here's something for you, Preacher. You're going to beat me there!"

And I would have squeezed the trigger over and over and over — and laughed. And wiped his blood on my friends' faces. And kicked his dead body into the filthy gutter. Now, the crowd stirs with emotion.

"There are too few David Wilkersons out on the streets tonight!" I proclaim. "Christianity has gotten too easy! It's scary out there, so we hide in here!"

And I tell of the most joyous moment in my life, when I led my mother to Jesus. How she changed so beautifully. How she served Him for 26 years — a respected and loved woman of God in rural Puerto Rico.

Of the wonderful happiness I feel when I know I'll spend eternity in Heaven with her.

My eyes full of tears, I stare across the auditorium. I'm startled to see that people are kneeling. Teens are blinking back tears. Little kids are hugging their parents.

My heart is filled to bursting. I see potential evangelists broken before the Lord, sobbing, their inner yearning for their Father reawakened.

"Will you serve Him?" I call out. "Are you willing to *fight* for Him in the streets? The final war has begun. We need reinforcements! Will you *die* for Him?"

The aisles are full. I pray with grandmothers and 10-year-olds and business executives and pastors.

"Yes," they answer, "we will fight. Show us how."

"I'll try," I whisper. "First step: Get your eyes off of me. Ask Jesus to show you how. He will."

That's such an important lesson for the maturing Christian warrior.

Men will fail you. We have faults — just like you do.

Fellowshipping with fellow Christians is immensely vital and will help you grow strong. Good Christian relationships are so important!

But only expect divinity of God.

No Christian is Christ. Men will let you down. And it'll hurt!

But Jesus will never fail.

Don's testimony

In the dingy darkness of the beach, the lay evangelist turned off the headlights of his $35,000 BMW coupe and waited. Over by the pilings of the pier, a swaggering kid strolled across the sand, stereo earphones over his baseball cap, his two-tone, hightop tennis shoes scuffing the trash-littered path.

"Hey," greeted the part-time evangelist in a soft southern drawl. He held out eight $5 bills. "How you doin', man."

It was the greeting of a baby boomer trying to be cool — lapsing into the lingo of his youth.

"No worries, Don," twanged the kid mockingly, digging into a pocket of his knee-length surfing shorts.

The evangelist fumbled with eight tiny glass vials the kid handed over. As far as the preacher was concerned, the conversation had ended. He was suddenly in a hurry. He backed his car away with a roar. In the moonlight, the young pusher squinted at the "JESUS Is My Co-Pilot" front license tag.

The kid sneered cynically. But the evangelist didn't hear. On a darkened parking lot, he was inserting "crack"—the rock cocaine he'd just bought—into a tobacco cigarette. Don excitedly inhaled its powerful smoke. He smiled in sudden peace. All was well. Everything was OK. Don's head rolled back against the headrest and he began to laugh to himself. His confidence had returned. *He felt good.* He felt powerful.

Don was what most people would call a success. He was a hard worker. He had pulled himself up by his bootstraps as the workaholic owner of a roofing firm, which he had struggled to build with his own hands — and with no financial backing. Then, he had taken his testimony onto the Christian dinner circuit. He was proud to call himself a "Yuppie" — a young, upwardly mobile professional. He drove very nice cars. His family lived in a sprawling, ranchstyle house on an expensive beachfront. He had two small daughters that were his particular joy. He had a wife who once had toiled in the hot sun on rooftop with him — before he had crews working for him and a fleet of trucks and two warehouses and a sheet metal shop.

Don's was a powerful testimony, delivered in a soft, friendly drawl when he was the special speaker at men's meetings.

In recent months, however, he had gotten caught up in the vicious cycle of keeping his testimony exciting and full of the amazing.

He'd begun lying about his financial successes. But people expected him to be immensely successful. He had to be a good witness, didn't he? He had to be able to tell bigger and better stories of God's amazing power and blessing.

Don had begun borrowing other people's stories of miracles. He would embellish the details just a bit, so that the stories became his.

Someone else's little girl on crutches became Don's grandmother in a wheelchair. Her twisted foot that was straightened became a stunted arm that grew out four inches.

But the powerful testimony was the same, he told himself. People's faiths were strengthened by the fabulous tales of spectacular moves of the Lord.

Yet, now Don sat alone on the beach, his mind writhing painfully in the on-again, off-again pleasure of his addiction — and the immense guilt that came with its ecstasy. Don knew that smoking crack was wrong. But he had grown up around drugs. Some months before, he'd made his choice to nurture this *one* little sin. It didn't hurt anybody else, he told himself. Plus, he needed the high.

But it became expensive. Pursuing it over the next months, he quietly drained his small cash reserves.

Increasingly he needed $40-50 worth daily to stay on an even keel as he dealt with the pressure of keeping his roofing crews working on schedule, as he bid on new jobs and as he hustled to bring his estimates in lower than those of the competition. Plus, he had his ministry — which dominated his weekends.

And then Don developed another problem. He really preferred the high that came from "free-basing." That was a lot more expensive and required him to juggle a small blowtorch and highly volatile chemicals to make the cocaine deliver a stronger punch.

Yes, he knew that free-basing had killed comedian John Belushi.

He had heard how actor Richard Pryor had become a human torch when the chemicals had exploded — and how rebuilding Pryor's face had taken months of plastic surgery.

Don had prayed about his cocaine problem. He felt very strongly that God had said it was OK. *Well ...*

Don would admit that God didn't actually tell him that it was OK. Don had just had a reassuring *feeling* that God still loved him and would put up with the addiction temporarily.

That wasn't altogether accurate. If you pressed him, Don would have confessed that God hadn't exactly said He would "put up" with the addiction.

The Lord had ... well, not declared that He would **strike Don dead** if he didn't quit using it.

Plus, Don would have explained, it was only a temporary sin. And it wasn't hurting anybody.

Often Don tried to talk to God while under cocaine's influence. When he did, the prayers were not as free or as full of joy as when Don had been a young Christian. Nevertheless, Don felt God heard him.

He knew God loved him.

But it was as if Don knew he was being left on his own — loved, but unprotected — as if God were quietly saying "I won't stop you from this private, self-destructive evil. But don't expect My blessing on your life while you're in rebellion against what you know is My will. And don't expect Me to shield you from the bad effects of your sin."

Would God have helped Don stop taking cocaine? Sure, Don knew, although the drug is incredibly addictive.

Some say that it can wrap a user in its tentacles after only one use. Quitting "cold turkey" is torturous and some professionals say a user is never free of a psychological dependency.

The gnawing craving for cocaine's chemically induced reassurance stays on. In moments of weakness and fear and inadequacy, one knows a little coke will make everything look better.

Yes, Don knew God could deliver him. Don had grown up in a large family in a very poor part of a large port city. His father had supported them by dealing in narcotics. Unlike TV and movie drug-selling jet setters enjoying the good life, Don's dad had been a very small-minded, vicious man who wasted his money and his life as he sold chemical death and fear to his customers.

Don had started getting drunk with his father and uncles perhaps as early as age three, begging sips of their drinks and performing hilariously while they laughed at his antics. He couldn't remember the first time he'd gotten high on marijuana. He could remember one time that his sister had blown smoke into the face of their baby brother and howled in mirth as the toddler careened around the apartment.

So, drugs had always been part of Don's life. But he'd never gotten addicted. That was something for fools and losers, his father had said time after time. Junkies were just the walking dead from whom you took thousands of dollars before their burial.

Don had sold lots of drugs as a youngster and a teen. He'd sold them to strangers and to friends — with whom he quit associating socially once the drugs took over their lives and they became thieves, burglars, muggers, prostitutes and petty con-men to support their habits. Then, while serving one of many short stints in jail — an unpleasant part of drug dealing — Don had heard about Jesus. He'd submitted his life to the Lord. He'd turned his back on his scoffing family and took up humiliating physical labor — as a minimum-wage roofer.

There he had met Julie — a former drug user who was working as a roofer, too. They had fallen in love. They had pledged their lives together to their Lord and Savior. And He had blessed their venture into business as they set up their own roofing crew.

Success had taken Don a long time. It was never easy. It required hard work, careful planning and intense concentration. So, Don started beating the hassles with a little of the stuff he had grown up with. When he tried crack, he felt a subtle warning that this one was too much—that he wouldn't be able to leave this one alone.

But he ignored the still, small voice. He felt he was in control. Just look at all that he had accomplished. Just look at his fascinating testimony — raised in a drug-dealing family, delivered by God's grace, blessed by financial success.

But Don's life began a slide that is difficult to explain to someone outside of the drug world. Don began getting high with friends whom he knew were stealing from him. Frequently, he stole from himself, breaking into his own warehouse to heist a piece of $700 equipment that he could trade for $100 worth of crack.

Then, one day everything that hadn't been stolen had been repossessed. Landlords had put liens on what remained for months of ignored rent. Julie had kicked him out of the house after she came home and caught him and several friends loading up the stereo. He'd been missing for a week, during which the microwave, VCR and large-screen TV had disappeared. It seemed that whenever Julie went out, she would return to find something else gone.

No, Don's drug use wasn't hurting anybody, he had said — hadn't he? It was a victimless crime — one that government needed to get its big nose out of, he felt.

You might be surprised that Don's story has a happy ending. But it took two years. Julie lost the house when she couldn't make the mortgage payments. She lost the cars. She lost everything except the living room furniture, which she moved into an unfurnished rental trailer that a member of their church found for her.

She tried working as a roofer, but was no longer suited for the coarse, hard life. Instead, she started cleaning houses — which paid surprisingly well.

Don disappeared for months at a time. He'd call from Colorado, Texas and Canada, offering reconciliation and asking for money. He actually tried checking himself into a couple of detoxification programs, but didn't have the thousands of dollars necessary to be admitted. All the time he sought the Lord—pleading for His mercy. And all the time God nudged his conscience: *quit depending on drugs, try depending on Me.*

"No," Don wept, "I'm not strong enough."

"That doesn't matter," the Lord spoke into his heart. "I am. Put your trust in Me."

Then Don went cold turkey. He did it alone and without friends on a beach in south Texas. He hitchhiked home. But Julie wouldn't even talk to him. She threatened to call the police when he tracked her down at one of her cleaning jobs.

She didn't believe his pleading promises that things would be different this time. Actually her heart did believe them — but her mind screamed, "No, Julie, no! How many times have you heard this before? How many times has he promised you the moon? How many times has he lied, using pious, Christian terms from his canned testimony to wrench your heart into giving in? No, Julie, no!"

Yet she did give in. As they knelt in the plain, tiny living room of the mobile home, Don begged forgiveness ... and Julie did, too ... and they again pledged everything to Jesus. Then they started all over again.

Did they live happily ever after? I believe they will. But struggles are ahead. Such is our Christian life. The walk of the obedient believer is never easy.

But greater is He that is in us than he that is in the world. Our hope is built on nothing less than Jesus Christ ... and righteousness. Just what can you or I learn from Don?

First, I would hope that leaders would see what happens when we push somebody into the ministry too quickly. We must avoid the mad rush to lift up new celebrity Christians before they have grown spiritually.

Second, I hope you can see that we cannot have little sins that "don't hurt anybody." Satan will trap you — just as he trapped Don with a little harmless high to get him through the day. Just as he snared King David standing up on the roof of his palace, peeking in at his neighbor's wife taking a bath.

Just as he trapped a Christian brother of yours and mine in the terrible filth of pornography. If you remember the news reports, this internationally respected teacher was drawn into an evil fascination with dirty pictures. Then, one day, he was caught at a sleezy motel where he had been photographing a prostitute. It was big news for the next week. For months, she didn't mind proclaiming to the world every detail of his sin.

We're all vulnerable to Satan's corrupting influences.

We each have weaknesses. The Lord has promised us that we will *have the strength to withstand* any sort of temptation — but Satan likes to push to that limit.

Sometimes it happens gradually.

It usually enters our lives very deceptively.

A little wine before bed each night. A little toke to loosen up with friends after work. A line of coke at a party — just as an experiment.

But it is always devastating and destructive if allowed to run its course. If you continue to live a life devoted to the pursuit of pleasure, you will be a lifelong searcher. As you devote yourself to satisfying the evil desires of your body, they will eventually master and control you.

And corrupt your influence. And your ministry.

And your soul.

But here is the dilemma. Don is not alone. Our church is full of Dons.

Not all of them take cocaine.

Putting our house
back in order

According to an article in the *Dallas Times Herald,* most Americans consider preachers to be dishonest, insincere, without any special relationship to God and especially untrustworthy with money.

Pollster George Gallup told a Minnesota Prayer Breakfast of 1,100 in St. Paul that the U.S. is suffering from a "deep spiritual malaise" — that there is a steep decline in trust of evangelists.

Perhaps you've read Ann Landers' classic column in which the housewife rushed around the house preparing for the pastor's visit. Jumping in the shower, she realized that she had forgotten coffee — and impulsively called her neighbor. "He'll be here any minute," she wailed, "can you run some over?"

"Sure," exclaimed the neighbor, "I'll dash across the lawn and meet you at the front door." Moments later, the doorbell rang. The housewife — still wearing what she'd had on in the shower — grabbed a dishtowel. Draping it in front of her, she threw open the door and declared:

"Oh, honey, I'm so glad you got here!"

Instead of a neighbor delivering coffee, on the porch stood the pastor, grabbing at his glasses. "Aghk," he stammered, turning toward his car, "I'll be back next week when I can bring my wife!"

That's not so funny when you've been a preacher. Such incidents are not all that common, but neither are they usually so innocent.

Many pastors simply will not visit after dark without their spouses. I know of one who used to take his kids, too — particularly whenever he had a midnight call from a woman who needed him to come over and counsel her.

I've visited one church which has a reputation of being a sort of Holy Ghost Hospital for disgraced pastors caught in sexual sin. The senior minister there went through a terrible time in his life in which he almost lost everything through a series of adulterous affairs. So, he understands when a fellow pastor shows up with his furniture in a U-Haul, the kids screaming in the back of the station wagon and his ashen-faced, betrayed wife biting her lip in the front seat.

Generally the ex-preachers go to work for a building contractor in the congregation — doing hard labor in the hot sun — for a year or so. Some have gone into contracting for themselves. Others return to the ministry — but only after long months of personal searching as they wander in their own private wildernesses, as they receive gentle restoration and as they enter a lifestyle of practical, daily holiness.

As I write this, the Church is in the midst of a new round of public humiliation of major evangelists and prominent teachers. Shocking sin is being broadcast for all to see and hear. I personally can tell you the worst is not over.

Several large ministries soon will be forced into the same fire — unless their leaders repent of financial sins, sexual errors, and deceptive practices. I say that partially as a prophet, but also as someone who has seen the sin firsthand. I am ashamed to tell you that in two cases in particular, I hesitated ... and hesitated ... and hesitated ... and just kept my troubled spirit to myself rather than confront the offenders. In one case, I refused to appear on this brother's TV show anymore. I did not like what I saw or heard.

But I did not feel that I knew him well enough to confront him. I am not used to playing the role of Jeremiah.

In the other case, I had been increasingly troubled that another fine brother's beautiful ministry was being corrupted by lust for power and money. No, I will not tell you this brother's name. But I am ashamed to admit that I waited and waited and waited. Then, I could wait no longer. I wrote him a long letter detailing my concerns. *What happened?*

His wife called me from a foreign country where the two were leading thousands to Jesus. She wept as she confessed

that I had discerned well. Then, my Christian brother got on
the phone and thanked me for caring. We prayed together. We
talked about God's forgiveness.

We talked about His unquenchable wrath toward those who
defy His authority and mock His laws.

Today, my fellow evangelist is still less than perfect. But I
see excellent signs that he took my brotherly warnings to
heart. I am continuing to pray for him and certainly to fellowship with him. Perhaps the Lord will use me further in this
mighty man's life. Or perhaps the Lord is preparing a word
for me from my brother.

I can only tell you that I could not sit back and do nothing
— while other ministries collapsed around us!

But, Nicky, you may be saying, what about Paul's warning
in Ephesians 5:3-7?

> *Let there be no sex sin, impurity or greed among you. Let
> no one be able to accuse you of any such things. Dirty sto-
> ries, foul talk and coarse jokes— these are not for you. In-
> stead, remind each other of God's goodness and be thank-
> ful. You can be sure of this: The kingdom of Christ and of
> God will never belong to anyone who is impure or greedy,
> for a greedy person is really an idol worshiper — he loves
> and worships the good things of this life more than God.
> Don't be fooled by those who try to excuse these sins, for the
> terrible wrath of God is upon all those who do them. Don't
> even associate with such people.*

Yes, I know deep in my hurting heart that this Scripture
must be taken very seriously. But note that it addresses the
unrepentant sinner.

If my Christian brother, the evangelist, was obviously defi-
ant of the Lord's authority and if he scoffed at the idea that
he ought to clean up his act, I would have no choice but to
disassociate myself. But when my brother is in the process of
recovery, I am not about to kick him in the teeth, denounce
him for past, forgiven sins or do anything else that might
cause him to stumble.

We have enough unrepentant sinners without humiliating
the ones who have turned from evil. Remember God's response to Ninevah's repentance.

He forgave even when Jonah did not.

Brothers and sisters, I cannot tell you how it makes me tremble as I see the new shame I believe Satan is planning to heap on Jesus Christ and His Church. I'm certainly not going to repeat what may be terrible, false rumors of sin.

But, I call you to be intercessors for our brothers and sisters. Truly terrible accusations are in the air.

Lord, I pray that these reports be lies! If they be true, Father, cause the offenders to fall on their knees before You in honest repentance! You have forgiven each one of us of terrible sins without forcing us to be shamed before our loved ones, our friends, our fellow Christians and certainly before the entire gawking world. So let it be again, Lord! You withheld your terrible judgment from Ninevah! Let it be the same today of Your servants, Lord! We know that You are a great God of forgiveness — You, indeed, always forgive sincere repentance!

So, Lord, spare these men and women of God that we Christians each love and respect and trust! Cause them to see their sins, if there be any, and to privately and humbly seek You anew! Yes, Lord! Spare this new humiliation that I see Satan has planned for Your people! Lead us to new holiness, Father. Cause us to yearn to be like You! In Jesus' name, I ask these things. Amen.

As I write this, my beloved wife, Gloria, keeps reading over my shoulder and whispering: "Love, Nicky, love. Don't write in anger! Teach in love." *She's so right.* Brothers and sisters, the Lord has laid a message of repentance and holiness upon my heart. God's love is mighty. He is so patient with us — despite our great sin — when we seek Him and humble ourselves before Him ... and obey Him.

However, I cannot remain silent any longer.

I have hesitated too long as it is.

I believe we are in danger of feeling God's terrible anger. Never forget what He did to the people of Noah's day. Yes, he has promised us never to destroy the world again with water. But, remember what He did to Sodom and Gomorrah many years after the flood.

Their sin was so great that Abraham could not find even

two righteous men. And so, God poured out His terrible wrath, obliterating the cities so completely and with such heavenly power that — tradition has it — today their former location is the lowest point on the face of the earth, the Dead Sea.

Also remember what He did to Ninevah.

After Jonah finally obeyed and preached God's anger, the people of Ninevah repented and turned to Jehovah. And our loving God held back His terrible judgment. Instead He blessed what had been a wicked and perverse nation!

Yes, Gloria is so right.

The answer is love.

Love. The love that drives a heartbroken mother to her knees in intercession for a rebellious teen.

True concern. A willingness to care.

Perhaps you doubt the effect of such prayer. Let me tell you a story about someone who took on such a burden. It's a tale that I heard some time back. I'm sorry that I don't remember all of the details nor the person's name.

Here's the story as it was told to me:

Jesus loves me, this I know…

The middle-aged lesbian was sick of life. She'd tried everything that it had to offer and was ready to put a revolver to her head and commit suicide.

As she cradled the pistol in her hands, she grew more and more fond of the idea of just finishing everything then and there. She wouldn't have to face her financial troubles — or her serious trouble with numerous VISA and MasterCard accounts and the IRS. She'd never have to go back to the job she hated, either, or her disappointing career. She would escape her abusive neighbors, her filthy apartment, her desperately unhappy search for companionship — and, well, the list went on and on.

Drugs hadn't been the answer to her deep unhappiness. Sex wasn't, either. Neither were the parties nor the bars nor the Eastern religions she'd tried — nor nine years of higher academics. Life had no meaning. It was a sick cosmic comedy. An opera poorly sung. A play without a worthwhile plot. *Now, she was ready to pull down the curtain.*

As she knelt in the bathtub of her apartment, she stared at the revolver, then looked up at the ceiling and asked no one in particular just why she shouldn't kill herself.

"The whole ——ing —— is just one —— bad joke," she cursed aloud. "I've ——ing tried *everything!*"

No, not everything, she realized suddenly. Somehow in the back of her mind, she began remembering the words of the children's ditty: *"Jesus loves me, this I know, for the Bible tells me so …."*

OK, I'll try that, she told herself.

But if it's just a sham, too, then I'm coming back here and finishing this job.

To make a long story short, she turned on her TV, searched for a "religious" show and found herself watching *The 700 Club.* The hour's feature story was interesting and had a Christian message. The host then explained the plan of salvation and led viewers through a prayer of repentance.

She whispered along. And began a new life.

This tale has an even more incredible ending. Would you believe this woman discovered some months later that a childhood friend had been praying for her *daily* for 25 years?

Upon returning to her hometown, she ran into her girlhood buddy and learned that her old comrade had for years had a godly burden for her.

Her friend had kept her on a lengthy daily prayer list — frequently moving her to the top of the list although they had lost contact years back.

The friend didn't know what she was praying for specifically — just that the Lord would bring her old friend into His kingdom.

Today, the woman credits her friend's prayers for saving her life. It was no coincidence, she says, that the words to *Jesus Loves Me* wafted through her mind at the moment she was ready to pull the trigger.

It was not "luck" that she turned on Christian TV and was immediately led through the sinner's prayer.

No, Satan had almost won after decades of plotting for her soul! He'd laid his traps carefully and she'd jumped willingly into most of them. Then, as he prepared a horrible place in hell for one more victim — AGHHHHHH! — the faithful prayers of a Christian warrior snatched the victory from him.

What had prompted those prayers?

Selfless love.

In her hard lifestyle, the woman had been difficult for anyone to love. She had hurt everyone who ever cared about her. She'd never asked for pity, much less for anyone to pray faithfully for 25 years on her behalf.

How can you or I love anyone like that?

How can we develop a burden for, say, Christian evangelists who have offended us? Or terrorists? Rapists in the state prison? People who cheat us? The teenager across the street who plays his demonic music at top volume when you're trying to take your Sunday afternoon nap?

The Scriptures tell us to do good to those who offend us. Sometimes, it's tempting to remember that by being good to our enemies, we heap "coals of fire" of guilt and confusion upon their heads, according to the Bible.

Well, if that's your motive, it won't work.

Instead, take his needs to the throne room of God and ask that he receive the Lord's greatest blessings — certainly including eternal salvation. Then, you have to be ready and willing should you receive the Lord's instructions to become a part of the solution.

Pray for your antagonist daily or even several times daily and you're going to see an incredible change in your attitude toward him or her. *You're going to care.* And that just may convict you about your critical spirit toward the person.

Try this, too: Do you have a serious problem with someone? Are you in strife with them? Did they offend you? Did they do something *really rotten?*

Don't try to be super-humble and selflessly pray for them. Don't list their sins to the Lord and pray for justice, either.

Instead, ask the Lord to forgive you both. *That's right.* No, it's not easy — particularly if you don't consider yourself guilty of anything. However, if you're really honest with yourself, you know that the other person probably has a completely different view of what happened to cause the strife.

So, ask the Lord to forgive you both. I guarantee that if you pray this in sincerity for at least a couple of days, you'll find your heart melting toward the brother against whom you have that grudge. You'll begin to see things a little bit from his side. And you won't be quite so adamant about your side of the fuss, either.

In fact, you may find the strength to obey Scriptural commands to go to the brother, apologize and get the matter resolved. *Why?* I know quite a number of reasons, but here's one of the best. Perhaps you love to quote Mark 11:22-24:

> *"...Jesus said to the disciples, 'If you only have faith in God—this is the absolute truth—you can say to this Mount*

*of Olives, 'Rise up and fall into the Mediterranean,' and your command will be obeyed. All that's required is that you really believe and have no doubt! Listen to me! You can pray for **anything**, and **if you believe, you have it;** it's yours!' "*

What a great promise! But read the verse that follows it — Mark 11:25:

"But when you are praying, first forgive anyone you are holding a grudge against, so that your Father in heaven will forgive you your sins, too."

Do you have a prayer list? A prayer journal? **Get one!** If you feel really strongly about something or someone, put the matter on your list. Pray daily about the situation. Seek the Lord's guidance. Ask Him to move the mountains that you, a mere human, cannot budge.

Can you, a prayer partner who stays at home, make a difference? The Apostle Paul seemed to think so. In Romans 15:30-33, he wrote to the Christians in Italy:

"Will you be my prayer partners? For the Lord Jesus Christ's sake, and because of your love for me—given to you by the Holy Spirit—pray much with me for my work. Pray that I will be protected in Jerusalem from those who are not Christians. Pray also that the Christians there will be willing to accept the money I am bringing them. Then I will be able to come to you with a happy heart by the will of God, and we can refresh each other. And now may our God, who gives peace, be with you all. Amen."

Do you know who else needs you as a prayer warrior?
Your pastor.

Friends, I'm not ashamed to proclaim that for every dishonest, hypocritical preacher or pastor or evangelist I meet, there are 100 sincere men of God hungering after God's truth, determined to win the lost. Few are anywhere close to being perfect. All are human. All have weaknesses. *All desperately need your and my fervent prayers.*

Prayers for what?

Strength and protection against fear and doubt. That's right. Today I see so many pastors who are terribly scared of failure — although they don't show it. So many are also scared that they don't have all the answers that you and I expect them to have 24 hours a day.

They are just human, too. Like you and me.

Pray for them! Love them! Remember that the vast majority gave up considerably more lucrative career opportunities to obey the Lord's call on their lives.

Ask the Lord to give them new peace and openness and freedom. And wisdom.

And *joy.*

And strength against the terrible temptations Satan loves to lay before God's leaders. Pray that they'll have protection from Satan's false accusers, too.

Prayer is such a powerful weapon. Many times, it's the only thing we can put to work!

Particularly if the burden on your heart is for an unsaved spouse. Or peace in Northern Ireland.

Or an end to world hunger.

Or for your church's great kids ...

Good Christian kids

Preaching isn't Jonathan's calling. He believes he is called of the Lord to work with Christian youngsters. A businessman during the week, he runs a weekend youth program in a large southeastern church whose several pastors have high national profiles and appear at numerous seminars, conventions and conferences.

Although he is just a volunteer, he oversees a large Sunday school, an enviable teen outreach program, an ambitious Junior Church and a weekly Family Night that includes BASIC for teens, and Pioneers Clubs, Bible Bowl, Whirlybirds, Junior Choir, Junior Orchestra and Young Dancers. However, he became quite disgruntled.

"This week," *he told his church's elders,* "the father of one of our more promising young men, a sixth grader, apologized to me for his son's bringing neighborhood troublemakers to church. The kids his son had brought were rude and disruptive. Since they caused his son to behave like a little jerk, too, the father told me that his son wouldn't bring them to church again."

He paused, frowning. The eldership meeting that night had attracted about 45 men. It had started off with its standard 30-minute time of praise, worship and exhortation — in which any man of the church could participate. Now it was in its problem-solving and business portion, which was run on sort of a roundtable basis — without strict parliamentary rules or *Robert's Rules of Order.*

Only the elders could vote, but anyone could speak up. The elders, including Jonathan, were elected by the other men.

"Men," Jonathan continued, "if that's our best solution, we've got some enormous spiritual problems which are going to keep this church from growing to its potential."

The church's ambitious growth plans were no secret.

"Can it be that we can only minister to *good little church kids*?" he asked. " I'm afraid that's the case right now. And we can barely handle them."

The youth program needed help, he declared — *the physical participation of more of the men helping out in class.* His request was met with silence. The men were not pleased with such a request — that they should teach little kids. They were the *men* of the church. The *elders.*

"Men," said Jonathan, "if we cannot take action to meet some of our deep needs, we need to quit bragging about our church's concern for our kids. We need to quit pretending that we are doing everything necessary to have a superb program. In fact, we currently have a deteriorating Wednesday night elementary school-age program since only a few will step forward to lead the necessary elements."

Repeatedly in past weeks he had brought to the board's attention the problem that two women were trying to run a Pioneers Club for 125 third, fourth, fifth and sixth graders — which Jonathan figured required a minimum of 15 workers to operate to its spiritual potential.

Yet his appeals for workers had fallen on deaf ears. The result was that the Pioneers Club was about to be discontinued. The two women were exhausted, burned out and increasingly frustrated with the serious discipline problems that occur when too few adults try to teach too many kids.

"We have a fine women's workshop on Wednesday nights," said Jonathan. "As a result, few of them want to help. And we have this superb eldership meeting — to which all the men of the church are invited. As a result, no men want to miss it and help with the kids."

"Yet, we are operating under a bit of selfishness."

Jonathan paused dramatically. He gazed out at the men.

"I believe it to be absolutely *preposterous* — if not a hideous lie straight from the deceiver," he said, his voice rising, "— for the men of this church to believe that the kids are the responsibility of the women!

"Please show me anything In the Old or New Testaments that supports that! Show me where young Samuel or 12-year-old Jesus went to meet with the women of the temple!

"Show me where young David was anointed and taught by the women!

"Friends, it did not happen!"

He paused to let his words sink in.

"We've been given some of the most remarkable youngsters I've ever dealt with. We are squandering the wealth of our future if we do not seek the Lord to find out where He would use each one of us to raise up the future leadership of this church."

The room was silent.

"I need you to help us out," he said. "I need men teachers. Role models — in classroom situations — for these youngsters, showing them how to worship, serve, love and bring others to God.

"Some of us are going to have to miss a few things we would like to attend. As it is, I hardly ever get to hear a sermon. But some of us are going to have to sacrifice just a little more. And I would appreciate it if it were some of you who haven't tried your hand at working with our incredible kids. I believe this could turn into a very fulfilling, ongoing ministry for you.

"A number of our own children are deeply starved for positive attention. It will warm your heart to find how easily you can make a big difference in their lives. I guarantee you won't be wasting your time with them. We've got some super kids and have been entrusted with a big responsibility to raise them up in the ways of the Lord."

How did the eldership board react? Jonathan was scolded for making an evil report. Jonathan — according to the other men — had come to them with condemnation, guilt, anger and a report worse than that of the Israelite spies who feared Canaan's giants.

The senior pastor told Jonathan that his timing was inappropriate — that if the problem was so severe, then the board should have heard of it long before. Then, the pastor noted there were a number of other things on the agenda that were more pressing and that it would be better if Jonathan brought the matter up in a more positive way at another time. Furthermore, the senior pastor said, he detected Jonathan was indeed much too angry over the whole thing.

Well, you can imagine that Jonathon was, indeed, angry after this meeting. He was also blind to an enormous failure on his part:

He had neglected to seek the Father's wisdom as he prepared to confront the men of the church. So, instead of recruiting an army, Jonathan just sounded an alarm that irritated the sleepy flock. *Sheep don't want to have to deal with wolves.*

They'd rather graze in the meadow.

The men of the eldership board didn't feel called to minister to little children. They much preferred discussing the budget, scheduling evangelism seminars and sitting in ego-boosting sessions where all was positive and they were continually praised for their leadership and spirituality.

Jonathan's heaping guilt on them in a fit of righteous frustration didn't really accomplish much. He charged into battle without any orders from his Commander and without any anointing.

So what did solve the problem? *Prayer.*

The children's program's problems began to be ironed out when Jonathan began *devoting himself to prayer* each morning for the kids of his church.

The Lord sent a group of women who began interceding as well. They beseeched the Lord to send the right workers, to touch the right consciences, to open the kids' hearts and to make the kids a top priority with the men and women of the church.

The result?

Spontaneously, a large number of men in the church began working with the children. Attendance in the youngsters' programs mushroomed. The church's attendence began a new boom as a result. Church kids brought unchurched kids who returned with parents, siblings, neighbors, uncles, aunts, schoolmates and grandparents. Sure, problems continued. But in the end, the victory was the Lord's.

Would prayer alone have solved this problem?

Or was there a need for somebody to sound the alarm?

Do you or I dare sound the alarm?

Do you ever sing the beautiful chorus "Alleluia"? It's the simple, gentle favorite that is merely the word "alleluia" repeated seven or eight times, sung to a gentle, worshipful melody.

Do you know who really wrote it?

One story has it that a group of Catholic sisters in Ohio were gathered in a prayer meeting and that the song just rose out of their hearts during a time of spontaneous praise.

However, a good Christian man in New York tells of seeking the Lord night and day for a "new song." The popular chorus suddenly welled up in his spirit as he was driving along the freeway, he says.

Believe it or not, there are quite a few versions of where this song originated. It has been transformed into a beautiful church musical by Bill and Gloria Gaither. The recorded verson sold hundreds of thousands of copies and was, I am told, the first Christian album to be "certified gold" by the record industry.

The truth of the matter is that the copyright is held by another Christian who has an even more inspiring story of how the song came to be written. I am prompted to marvel, after hearing all the stories, how this song was spread by our Father throughout His people in a beautiful and amazing way.

The song swept through our brotherhood, bringing with it healing, peace and a new desire to worship Him in reverence and holiness.

Thus it is with God's message to His people throughout history. Many hear God's voice. Some speak out. Others wait, then are filled with joy upon hearing the word confirmed through the words of other men and women.

Sometimes the message is that the trumpet must be sounded — even if the call into battle is not edifying or ego-boosting.

I have written this book because I believe that a number of urgent warnings must be issued to God's children today. They burn deeply in my heart. But I must write in God's wisdom and timing — or else you, the reader, will not hear what the Lord wants to be said, and what I believe He is causing to be said already in hearts and pulpits and other books across the world.

I don't want this book to be a "shocker." I want you to know that I have 3,000 people praying that the true message on the next 150 or so pages will be heard — and will be a confirmation of what you're already hearing ... or will soon be hearing. My soul trembles at the terrible possibility that some of you will just think this is one more Christian "scare" book warning of a terrible *human* conspiracy.

No. I trust that you will not misunderstand me. Perhaps it would help if you join me and my editors in taking this serious matter before the Lord:

"Father, open my heart and my eyes and my spirit to Nicky's simple message. He's just a man. He doesn't always use the right words. Sometimes his editors don't always get things right, either. But through the power of your mighty Spirit, help me *to understand. In Jesus' Name, Amen."*

Why do we offer such a prayer?

Psalm 127:1 gives us this warning: "... Unless the Lord protects a city, sentries do no good." That is, without intercession and prayerful seeking of the Lord's will, the alarm will not be heard. The flock will just be irritated.

God's people have a history of stoning prophets.

And the corrupter continues his ugly assault unopposed.

Without prayer — fervent on-your-knees prayer — expect mediocre results as you sound any alarm, if not outright failure. The prayer warrior takes earthly matters into the heavenlies. The battle becomes much more than struggles between flesh and blood. Angelic forces are sent in. The Lord joins the battle between good and evil. And guess who always wins? The true Master of the Universe, our God. Too often we see prayer as too simple a solution. It's too pat. *Too ordinary.* It's also hard work — a truth that many of us would rather not admit. We'd rather take things into our own human hands. We go into earthly action — *when we should linger on our knees.* How then, should we sound the alarm?

There are two different methods of alarm-sounding in Numbers 13: 27-14:9. First, the ten doubting Israelite spies reported in one manner; then the two faithful ones, Joshua and Caleb, took a different tack.

If you remember, Moses had sent them all into the Promised Land to find out what lay ahead.

First, the report of the ten:

> *"We arrived in the land you sent us to see, and it is indeed a magnificent country—a land flowing with milk and honey. Here is some fruit we have brought as proof. But the people living there are powerful, and their cities are fortified and very large; and what's more, we saw Anakim giants there! The Amalekites live in the south, while in the hill country there are the Hittites, Jebusites, and Amorites; down along the coast of the Mediterranean Sea and in the Jordan River valley are the Canaanites ...."*

Here's how fellow spy Caleb responded:

> *"Let us go up at once and possess it for we are well able to conquer it!"*

To which the other spies retorted:

> *"Not against people as strong as they are! They would crush us! The land is full of warriors, the people are powerfully built, and we saw some of the Anakim there, descendants of the ancient race of giants. We felt like grasshoppers before them, they were so tall."*

To which Caleb and Joshua thundered:

> *"It is a wonderful country ahead, and the Lord loves us. He will bring us safely into the land and give it to us. It is very fertile, a land flowing with milk and honey! Oh, do not rebel against the Lord, and do not fear the people of the*

land. For they are but bread for us to eat! The Lord is with us and he has removed his protection from them! Don't be afraid of them!"

Did Joshua and Caleb ignore the problems? *No!*

They acknowledged that a challenge lay ahead — but offered a plan of action, noted the Lord's power, as well as His command to enter the land, and cautioned against fear.

I believe that's how we're to deal with problems. That's what I hope to do in this book, too. We must call for action. But we must seek the Lord's solution and offer it hand-in-hand with our unveiling of the problem. We aren't much help if we just become a new part of the problem.

Instead, let's be a part of the solution.

How? *We must seek the Lord before we take action.*

Listen for His instructions. That gentle nudge on your heart. That reassurance in your Spirit. That exciting release to go ahead. Or that calming, gentle urge to wait.

Many times the Lord knows things that we cannot see. He is never deceived by men's devices.

Trust Him.

Wait on Him to show you whether to hurry into the Promised Land.

Or to be cautious of something that is *not* what it appears to be.

Why must we speak out in wisdom and love?

Closed circuit cameras prowl a highly lit mail room at a large Christian ministry. There, hundreds of thousands of letters are efficiently opened and the money removed. Conveyor belts move the envelopes and correspondence into another room. Workers at computer screens pull letters off of the assembly line and hit the appropriate buttons on their keyboards to produce "personal" responses to the letters.

For example, one letter from, let's say, John and Jane Horowitz, asks healing for "Amy." The keypunch operator types in the Horowitz's names, "healing" and scans the letter, but can't find any clue as to who Amy is. So, the worker hits the buttons for "loved one" and "female." Then the worker types in the word "Amy" and goes on to another letter.

As she does, the ministry's large computer is churning out thousands of letters. Down in the midst of the pile is this "personal note" to Mr. and Mrs. Horowitz — one of thousands that resulted from the few moments that keypunch operators spent scanning the incoming mail:

Dearest Partners John and Jane Horowitz:

*My beloved wife and I were so glad to get your good letter today here at our international prayer room. We are **so** concerned about Amy.*

Our ministry depends on faithful friends such as you, people that we can depend on for our deep financial needs. I said to my wife, thank Jesus for people like the Horowitzes — and thank Jesus that we can pray for their Amy.

I want you to know that my wife and I have asked the Lord to miraculously provide your loved one's healing —

yes, to answer our fervent prayers concerning Amy. And now, again, we come before the throne of the Almighty.

Lord, you know Amy's situation. In faith believing, we speak healing into Amy's life. Healing, Lord, in the name of Jesus of Nazareth. Amen and amen.

Before I close, I just want to let you know that as I was praying for Amy's healing, I felt the Lord assuring me that you are going to be a part of our great miracle to raise $12 million for our new broadcast studio. The Lord is telling you to send at least $100 — although the sacrifice may be great. The promise is wondrous. And the fields are white unto harvest. I know we can depend on your faithfulness as we have so many times before. Praise God for friends such as the Horowitzes.

In His service, Your friend and partner ...

If you've gotten such letters, you may have already suspected that *something* is not quite as it seems. But, is there anything wrong with an evangelist *pretending* to be your faithful pen pal? Is there anything sinful about his telling you that he is praying about your needs when, in fact, he never sees your letter?

Should you or I speak out against what we believe is deception?

Is it OK — since his is a divine and righteous cause — for this teacher to tell you that, as he was praying for you, the Lord told him a specific cash amount you should send ... when, in fact, he did not pray for you and the Lord did not speak to him?

What does the Bible say?

Consider the Apostle Paul's words to the church in Corinth on the subject of letters that he had written to them:

"We are so glad that we can say with utter honesty that in all our dealings we have been pure and sincere, quietly depending upon the Lord for his help, and not on our own skills. And that is even more true, if possible, about the way we have acted toward you. My letters have been straightforward and sincere; nothing is written between the lines!" (II Cor. 1:12-13)

Honesty. **Sincere.** Quietly depending upon the Lord for His help. *Straightforward.*

Nothing written between the lines.

Now, go back and read that computer-generated letter. As you can see, everything about it is a terrible, absolute lie.

Furthermore the preacher who writes this sort of letter gets on TV and tells viewers that he and his wife pray over each and every letter! Friends, with my small ministry, I cannot pretend to be able to read all the mail that comes in. I have good Christian staffers who read everything. Frequently they will give me a letter that requires my special attention. But when I send out a letter that has a personal message or advice or an assurance that I am praying about a matter, *be assured that I am doing just that!*

I know it grieves you when you see these lying letters on the coffee tables of good, trusting friends — who do not suspect that the letter is an absolute sham.

I am sure we both know faithful donors who actually believe they are personal friends and weekly pen pals with the people who send out these letters — and that their personal needs are a matter of daily prayer for the evangelist and his wife and international staff.

I've seen these shamelessly computer-generated, computer-signed letters actually framed on believers' walls — as prized possessions!

What should you or I do?

Frankly, I rarely open my mouth to inform such donors of the truth. They would be crushed to learn that the whole thing is a lie. It would hurt too much. But this deception is an abomination straight from hell — a deception slicker than any sham dreamed up by Madison Avenue. *A lie!*

And here is the terrible part. One evangelist regularly is visited by these "pen pals" — who are expecting him to spend time with them.

But since he is such a busy minister of the Gospel, he refuses to see any of them as a matter of policy! I can say this because his local newspaper from time to time prints the heart-breaking story of the latest incident. One I remember was a grandmother from Taiwan — the Republic of China — who spent every cent she owned to come and bring her prayer request to him in person. Yet, he would not see her — even when the incident generated terrible local publicity! His response was that he wasn't going to be pushed around by the ungodly news media.

And what about this boldfaced falsehood that during prayer for Amy's healing *that the evangelist was told by God* that these folks should send $100?

Hundreds of thousands of such letters go out —printed by a computer! Did the Lord tell the computer during its prayer time that the donor should send $100?

No! Of course not! How can the Lord continue to bless a ministry that is built on such *lies?* Some ministries have such sophisticated computer systems that individuals' past donations are carefully evaluated so that the computer can set a reasonable appeal for each "partner."

I know of a man and wife who carefully saved up $500 to repair their porch. Then, they got a letter from their favorite computerized pen pal who said that the Lord had told him that they should mail him $1,000. These folks were crushed. They would have to borrow the other $500. But they dared not disobey a word from the Lord!

How many times have you been offended by an obviously deceptive appeal for money? How many times have you written to the author, telling that you will not send another cent because you have this or that problem with his techniques or message or lifestyle?

Probably, you have never done this!

Are you justified in objecting to extravagance? Jesus constantly rebuked the religious showmen of his day!

"They love to wear the robes of the rich and scholarly, and to have everyone bow to them as they walk through the markets. They alove to sit in the best seats inthe syunagogues, and at the places of honor at banquets — but they shamelessly cheat widows out of their homes and then, to cover up the kind of men they really are, they pretend to be pious by praying long prayers in public. Beware of this, their punishment will be the greater!" (Mark 12:38-40)

"You wear a noble, pious expression in public, but God knows your evil hearts. Your pretense brings you honor from the people, but it is an abomination in the sight of God." (Luke 16:15)

Why should you write to those who send you offensive appeals for cash?

Believe it or not, only about 1 percent of direct-mail recipients respond. The other 99 percent just ignore the letters. So, what if you or I wrote a friendly note explaining *why* we were not sending a donation — but that we would be drenching our brother or sister in daily prayer? I believe that many of these ministries would re-evaluate what they're doing. They might ignore the letters. But God will not ignore the prayers.

Many of these "urgent" appeals for donations are prepared by hired specialists — companies that specialize in this sort of thing and who brag about their ability to create appeals that "pull" donations better than others. I have seen times when the "crisis" is concocted since many Christians today will respond only to emergencies. As I noted, the appeals are sent out knowing that only 1 percent of the recipients will respond. Yet, the 1 percent send in enough cash to pay for the hundreds of thousands of letters mailed — as well as raise additional money.

Such poor response no longer concerns some of these ministries. They are delighted with a 4 percent response. The direct-mail, fund-raising technique is just a numbers game. You spend $20,000 to mail out 100,000 direct mail letters. One percent — 1,000 folks — respond with gifts averaging $30. So, the campaign is a success. It pulled in $10,000 more than the ministry started out with.

So, I repeat, next time you get an offensive appeal for cash, send a letter and explain why are offended by the mail you were sent. Should you send a donation? Take it before the Lord. Ask the Father. It's His money, after all, right? Anything that any of us has really belongs to the Lord of our life, right? I hope so. I try to practice that in my own life — although it's not always easy.

Write in love — not condemnation. Show our brothers that we care about them and that we are united with them in feeding the sheep and reaching a lost world. Then, remembering how Christ is gentle and patient with you, mention your concern. Share appropriate scriptures.

Pray over the letter before you send it. Pray that it reaches the right person and is not tossed away as crank mail. *If God could guide the Israelites through the Sinai for 40 years, He can guide your letter into the right hands.*

The seduction of the Horror Gospel

My Christian brother, David Wilkerson, was recently called by God to go warn a prominent evangelist to step down and take time to be alone with the Lord. The evangelist told Dave his commitments made that impossible. Saddened, Wilkerson repeated that this was a word from the Lord — not just something that Dave thought ought to be said.

And within weeks, this evangelist was on all the news shows, in all the newspapers — and being ridiculed by editorial cartoonists and talk show comics. In humiliation, he stepped down from his high place — just as Wilkerson told him the Lord wanted him to do. But this time, it was not by his choice. *What a shame when you or I hear from our own personal Nathan, yet refuse to obey.*

And what a terrible thing when you or I begin to believe that we are God's greatest spokesmen, that everything has been entrusted to our hands, and that we are the ones who are accomplishing great things for God.

This is when the Lord steps back from us.

And he allows the evil hounds of hell to humble us.

When God sends his prophet to warn us, the message must be taken to heart in prayer. We must humble ourselves before the Lord, seeking his guidance and direction. God has placed in each and every one of us what I call a warning system. We are His sheep and His sheep know His voice.

However, Satan tempts us with the applause, the glory and all the praise of men until we believe that we can do no wrong.

That's what happened to another one of the major evangelists who fell. Insiders have told me that he honestly believed that he could do no wrong. When he fell into a sexual trap, he just laughed it off. He was God's anointed, he felt. No evil would befall him. *He was wrong.*

As a minister's audience dries up, he either grows more determined to seek out and find the Lord, or he begins giving in to the seduction of switching to more appealing, ear-tickling topics. If that happens, I believe the Lord removes His blessing from a ministry. The anointing may remain on the minister's life. The gift remains. But the power leaves his sermons and ministry.

What happens when a pastor tries to fake the anointing? What happens when the Lord no longer gives him the words to say or brings him the crowds? The easiest temptation is to take matters into one's own hands with hype, hoopla and deception.

You become a clever storyteller with only the stalest second-hand messages to impart at the punchline of your dramatic tales. You turn into a Christian comic with a hilarious presentation but little or nothing to speak into people's lives.

Immense financial problems often surface. Embarrassing sin is exposed. Yet, you begin manipulating the unsuspecting masses into complacency — "God likes you just the way you are! You're His creation and He don't make no trash! — Feel good about yourself! I like you and God does, too."

You begin offering them false ways to atone for their sins: "God is going to fix up everything in your life today if you'll plant a seed of faith by calling in your VISA or MasterCard number to me right now."

You begin stirring their emotions with the shocking revelation of the week. Have you heard the rumor that the Federal Communications Commission is going to shut down Christian radio stations across America — unless Christians flood FCC offices with petitions? That's a favorite of some small time revival preachers.

Yet, those reports are absolutely false! Yet in the last 12 years, 20 million petitions, postcards and letters from Christians have flooded FCC offices. The rumor apparently is perpetuated by one particularly atheistic outfit in Texas, "leaked" to various alarmist or naive Christians on a regular basis and spread by those who hear and believe. The atheists then laugh in glee at how stupid they make the Christians look.

Figure postage spent and you see Christians have been worked into a lather by ministers who stirred them to waste at least $4 million to stop something that never existed. The fact is that the FCC has no plans to take religious programming off the air. "And even if it did, under the wildest stretches of imagination, the First Amendment would forbid it," FCC spokesman John Kamp told the *Associated Press.*

How about the shocking stories that a popular hamburger chain and a large household products corporation were both owned by satanists? Totally untrue. But the reports were *so* exciting.

How about the notion that the UPC bar-code symbols on grocery items are the Mark of the Beast? Even today, many Christian publishers won't allow the UPC symbols on their products — not because they believe the absurd notion that the bar-codes are demonic, but because they don't want to run the risk of being denounced by the professional Christian finger-pointers who run to and fro across the earth stirring up fear.

How about fear of displaying God's symbol to Noah — the rainbow? Several authors have declared that anyone displaying the heavenly sign of God's promise is a secret agent of the New Age movement. *I'm not exaggerating this claim.*

This preposterous idea was that New Agers hidden in the Church signal their presence to one other with this secret talisman — the rainbow. Thus, anyone with a bumper sticker bearing a rainbow and the message "God Loves You" is probably a secret Hindu/witch/nephilim eager to teach yoga in church schools, sell health food in the parsonage basement and fill Christian music with demonic backward masking.

Absurd. Yet, when a pastor or a TV evangelist is corrupted by a lust for applause, adoration, worship of millions, fame, superstardom, power and the praise of men, incredible absurdities are passed off as the message of the Lord.

The seduction to begin preaching half-true horror tales is only one result. The worst is that the message of God's love and redeeming power gets corrupted, twisted and forgotten.

I believe that if the Lord puts a message on your heart, He

will provide you with the means to deliver it to those who need to hear. What if the thousands of dollars for TV time don't roll in? Then perhaps the Lord has something else for you — out of the limelight.

Maybe a local pastorate. Maybe a ministry to street people. Perhaps a job in the secular world where you can witness to co-workers. Or maybe a time of rest—completely out of active, energetic ministry for a season.

Aren't emotional appeals for money critical to the success of a ministry? No! They are a symptom the minister has serious spiritual problems he must address before he is tempted into trying other human techniques to attract an audience and its donations.

Behind the scenes, I find desperation at so many ministries. They are dependent on millions of dollars coming in weekly. To keep the dollars coming in, new emergencies, *gimmicks* and building projects must be created. The building project cycle is one of the worst traps ministries get into. People will donate money to build this or that tower or dorm or studio — particularly if viewers are told the building won't get built unless they give.

Yet, and this troubles me greatly, many times the donations pulled in by such urgent appeals are actually used to keep the ministry on the air. Certainly a portion is used to build the new structure.

But, the ministry is caught in a trap of build or perish. I know of one ministry in particular whose leader seems on the verge of despair whenever I meet with him privately. He can't quit building. Why? People will quit giving if he does — and much of his income results from appealing for money for the building projects. Many of his existing buildings are in disrepair, but there's little in the budget for maintenance. The gaudy structures were built cheaply and won't last 20 years. They're designed to look beautiful on a TV screen — but have immense amounts of wasted interior space.

Yet, he must continue to build new ones and appeal for the money to build them — although his heart really isn't in it anymore. I believe that very soon, we will see such ministries falter and collapse.

It has already begun.

Their deception and waste have begun to be exposed. Believers have begun to turn their backs. In shame, the Church will cease to mention their names or admit having been deceived. The deceptive money mills will have been a passing thing in the history of Christianity — the corrupted money ministries of the 1960s, '70s and '80s.

Thank God that there are legitimate ministries spreading the Gospel. I encourage you to support them. The Lord has given you discernment for a reason. Let's not throw the baby out with the bath water. TV is one of the most effective evangelism tools ever offered to God's people.

But we can't just pretend that there have not been corruptions. No, today, we still have a problem — and we must do something about it.

If we don't somebody else will. Who?

You may have noticed, secular TV has become no longer content merely to woo away our children with its sex, violence, rebellion and magic. It is beginning to tear down our temples and send our not-so-innocent leaders into exile. The gossip-mongering supermarket tabloids are tired of Jackie O and Liz and Patty Hearst and soap opera actors. *They've discovered there's great reader interest in the sins of the holy!*

Even the legitimate press clamors to win Pulitzers for proving in shocking detail that this man of God or this woman with a mighty ministry is a tithes-pilfering hypocrite practicing shocking sin.

Why is the press having to clean up our house for us? *Because we Christians did nothing!* When we saw sin, we looked the other way and made excuses for those we loved and trusted!

So, the Lord used the evening news to do our job. Instead of confronting our brothers and saving them from the humiliation of being exposed by unbelievers, we just closed our eyes. ***We did nothing about the sin in our midst.*** God told us in our hearts that something was terribly wrong, but we closed our eyes and our ears and pretended that nothing was troubling our spirits so deeply.

In our disobedience, we *wanted to feel good!* But we wanted no discipline. Certainly no holiness. In our "bless me, bless me" selfishness, we ignored the prophets calling us to join our

Father out in the wilderness! We made up excuses about dishonest fund-raising gimicks. We closed our ears and did not
speak out when God urged us to be Nathans and Elijahs!

We waited and waited and waited —

And then, God sent modern-day Babylon to come in and
take our young men off into captivity. Our sin was such a
stench in our Lord's nostrils that He used God-mocking, scoffing, authority-defying, money-centered, humanistic gossip-
spreaders to clean out the idolators and prostitutes and mon-
ey-changers shaming His holy temple!

"That's pretty strong stuff, Nicky," you may be saying to
yourself.

Yes. But when ancient Israel refused to return to God, the
evil Babylonians were allowed to come in and plunder the cities, destroy God's temple and take the brightest and the best
into exile. Read the Book of Daniel. The Lord God's finest,
most faithful young men of Israel were taken hostage by one
of the most evil civilizations ever to defile humanity. The
Lord did not turn back the evil invaders until His people fell
before Him in repentance and sorrow—and threw down their
idols, turned from their evil and returned to His way.

**Today, God wants a clean and strong body of believ-
ers.** I don't believe for a minute that all the recent scandals in
the press have been the work of Satan to destroy good men. I
believe that our Lord has used some unlikely agents in the
news media to perform the same job that was given to the
wicked kings of Babylon, Assyria and Persia — to chastize
the people of God.

What is the answer to all of this? We must return to the
simplicity of Jesus' message! The Lord orders us to go unto all
the world and set up Holy Ghost Hospitals! Places of spiritual
healing and restoration.

"But, Nicky," you may protest, "you have too much compas-
sion for the wolves preying on our Church's sheep! Satan's
evil angels are enjoying an open season in our pastures! It's
time to denounce the wicked, banish the pretenders, and send
the false prophets out into disgrace and ruin!"

Well, how does the Bible tell us to go about doing that?

How are we to root out evil in our midst?

We have simple rules for exposing evil in our midst

Mary grew up at a newspaper. As the teenage copygirl, she was occasionally allowed to do short articles. One day, she was given a clipping from another newspaper in which a prominent local physician was quoted as endorsing euthanasia — mercy killing of terminally ill patients.

Eager to show off her writing skills, my friend rewrote the piece for her newspaper. Proudly she took the article to her boss, a crusty assistant city editor.

Fifteen minutes later, the boss waved down the copygirl. "Pretty good writing," said the editor. "What did the doctor say to you?"

"Oh, I didn't call him," said Mary, "I just rewrote the other article. It looked pretty good."

"Hmmm," said the editor. "Well, I called him. Tomorrow morning he's suing the other newspaper. He denies that he ever said any of this."

The copygirl was stunned. She had not checked her facts. She had almost involved the newspaper in an ugly lawsuit. Fortunately, she had a boss who had the good sense to pick up a telephone and ask some questions when it seemed unlikely that a prominent doctor would make such statements.

Why can't the Church at least have the standards of the ungodly news media? Today, many Christian alarm-sounders skip vital steps. In their rashness, I believe they rationalize away any need for the Bible's guidelines for accusing the brethren.

But Jesus gave us clear biblical steps for correcting a Christian who is sinning. The accuser must meet with the offending brother and find out if, indeed, evil is being practiced unrepentantly — or if the accuser has bad information or has misjudged. That's exactly what has happened in so many of these popular books. Authors shoot from the hip — refusing to even verify whether the accused stands by printed statements.

I know of one book manuscript in which a Christian pastor was accused by name on the basis of a newspaper account of a radio interview!

As hard as it is to believe, did the author call the pastor and ask if he had been quoted properly in the nonchristian press?

NO! Did the author ask the pastor if the quote was in context or reflected the way he now believes? NO! Did the author even give the pastor the courtesy of explaining his position? NO! No contact was made! The first time the pastor saw the accusation was when it appeared in in the book!

When confronted about such sloppy editorial practices in a book that his company had published, one Christian publisher responded that "everyone knew" the accused was guilty.

Just who is "everybody?" Don't our Christian leaders have the same rights as common criminals — to face their accusers and be presumed innocent until proven guilty?

One Christian group attacked in that book was an international ministry to the starving. Its leader was quoted using terms also used by New Age occultists. After the book came out, donations dropped dramatically — although the leader tearfully denied any involvement with the New Age movement and denied he had been guilty of anything more than using terms such as "global village," "Spaceship Earth" and "networking" in a magazine article on world hunger.

What a tragedy! Just because men of God cannot obey His rules for confronting each other!

How must we accuse the brethren? Face-to-face. One-on-one. In private. If the accused will not change, then you and I are supposed to take someone else with us and confront the offender again. If that is ineffective, we are to take the matter up before a local congregation.

Why all this trouble? Because there's always a possibility that you or I are making false and irresponsible accusations — and that arguments from both sides need to be heard in private long before we open fire on each other in public. Consider that ministry to the starving. When the accusing book became a best-seller, volunteers were devastated by the charges. How could anyone with an ounce of spiritual discernment believe that their leader's use of "New Age words" proved that their respected charity was in league with Satan?

It, of course, was no proof at all. If you or I refer to "redistribution of wealth," does this make us communist one-worlders dedicated to destroying the Church and instituting a worldwide monetary system?

No, of course not. How silly. The leader's use of those terms meant he thought they had a catchy ring and was unaware they were offensive to some people — not that he had thrown years of heart-felt conservative conviction out the door and now had become a card-carrying commie in search of an airliner to hijack.

Enormous damage was done to a respected Christian ministry just because one author failed to obey our Lord's commandments. Yet, to this day, no apology has been issued. The book continues to sell by the thousands. And the damage mounts.

This backstabbing among Christians must stop. You and I must guard ourselves not to be guilty of gossip-mongering. Don't buy the books that point fingers. Don't support name-callers financially. Get up and walk out of seminars where Christians begin listing Christian offenders by name. If challenged, cite Galatians 6:1-3:

> *"Dear Brothers, if a Christian is overcome by some sin, you who are godly should gently and humbly help him back onto the right path, remembering that next time it might be one of you who is in the wrong. Share each other's troubles and problems, and so obey our Lord's command. If anyone thinks he is too great to stoop to this, he is fooling himself.* **He is really a nobody.**"

Demonstrate your disapproval. Don't join the ugly battle. This is particularly true today when the gawking, mocking, ungodly media is ready to chronicle the latest verbal exchanges in what they like to call our "Holy Wars." Just look at all the fun the press had with Jim and Tammy Faye Bakker and Jerry Falwell — particularly in the beginning when it looked as if Jimmy Swaggart, Pat Boone, John Ankerburg, James Robison and the entire Assemblies of God denomimation could be dragged into the muddy brawl.

Then we had to endure it all over again when a brother offended by another prompted the terrible chain of events that humiliated Jimmy Swaggart. Do you know what I think was the worst part? When God's leaders glibly began taking verbal blasts at each other on national TV. Who is truly degraded? Our Lord.

Remember what a wonderful time the media had with Jimmy Carter's admission that he had lusted in his heart? Or that hurricane-denouncing Pat Robertson had not been celibate before giving his life to Jesus. Or that Ronald Reagan actually believed there would be a Battle of Armageddon ... and then that he practiced astrology after espousing so many causes of concerned Christians.

Notice, too, how the media loves to chronicle pastors caught in sex sin. Newspapers detail the shame of every priest accused of molestation and every pastor caught in adultery. Mockingly the press parades these new examples that Christianity doesn't work and that men of God are hideous hypocrites.

We have to be careful in taking accusations of the brethren into the brutal public arena. We must expose sin within our midst. But we must obey God's strict rules for doing it. Why? Because sometimes you and I are wrong as we point our fingers in gossip and accusation. We must be very careful — particularly when we consider the warning in Proverbs 6:16-19:

> *"There are six things the Lord hates—no, seven: haughtiness, lying, murdering, plotting evil, eagerness to do wrong, a false witness, sowing discord among brothers."*

We're never permitted to talk badly about an offender. Gossiping is listed right up there with murder and whoremongering. Read Romans 1:28, for example:

> *"So it was that when they gave God up and would not even acknowledge him, God gave them up to doing every-*

*thing their evil minds could think of. Their lives became
full of every kind of wickedness and sin, of greed and hate,
envy, murder, fighting, lying, bitterness, and gossip ...."*

So, let's not be guilty of just sitting back and criticizing.
We're not given that option, brothers and sisters. Romans
14:10-13 is blunt:

> *You have no right to criticize your brother or look down
> on him. Remember, each of us will stand personally before
> the Judgment Seat of God. For it is written, "As I live,"
> says the Lord, "every knee shall bow to me and every
> tongue confess to God." Yes, each of us will give an account
> of himself to God. So don't criticize each other any more.
> Try instead to live in such a way that you will never make
> your brother stumble by letting him see you doing some-
> thing he thinks is wrong.*

It is so easy to just become Pharisees — sneering and pointing accusing fingers and shaking our heads in dismay.

But we — you and I — must confront the offenders.

We cannot just ignore the problem. There is still time for
Christians to put our own house in order. Sure, we are concerned that the Church is ailing. Both good and bad doctors
have examined the patient and pronounced it in need of intensive care. But, what can we do?

By doing nothing, we surrender to Satan's tactics. We say
that our God can't change our brothers' hearts nor remove the
blinders on their eyes nor do anything about the generally
terrible state of affairs — which is, of course, not true.

What if you are not a letter-writer? Can you fast?

"But Nicky," you might protest, "my pastor says that fasting is only for times of grieving and desperation — when
nothing else has worked."

Dear friend, look around you. Our wonderful, loving modern Church too often is a bragging, bickering, finger-pointing,
man-centered, legalistic, undisciplined collection of spiritual
dwarfs demanding to be fed — but turning down meat and
screaming for more milk!

It's time to pray. *It's time to fast.* It's time to wage spiritual
war.

"Oh, come on, Nicky," you may be saying now, "I love my local church. It's where I get my weekly dose of spiritual encouragement. It's where I get the fellowship I so desperately need. I love my pastor. Under his teaching, I am just beginning to understand the deeper things of God. Things can't be as bad as you make them out."

Don't quit going to church. I, too, belong to a fine congregation — Radiant Church in Colorado Springs, Colorado — where I learn new things constantly, where I fellowship with brothers and sisters without whom my life would be empty indeed. Listen, I believe that we evangelists can get ourselves into untold trouble when we are not under anyone's authority, lack the spiritual backup of Christian brothers and sisters, and when we attempt to function as spiritual supermen answerable only to God.

I've placed myself under submission to my pastor, Don Steiger, and I am grateful for his frequent input into my life. Although I do not limit my ministry to churches or groups of any one denomination, I maintain and value my credentials with the Assemblies of God — particularly because of the high standards that this group requires of pastors and evangelists.

So, please do not misunderstand my words.

The local church is vital. Your attendance is mandatory for you to be in obedience and to develop as a mature Christian. In fellowship with one another we Christians can grow strong in the love of the Lord. Under good teachers, we reach higher in wisdom and knowledge of the Word of the Lord. And amid corporate praise and worship, we see His mighty presence among us.

But don't let your contentment with your blessings keep you from being a spiritual warrior. It's time to put on our Christian armor and march into battle!

How? On our knees.

Yes, it is time for each of us to look at the corruption within our ranks. No, we cannot just look the other way. But the sin must be dealt with — according to God's ways, not our own. Brothers and sisters, pray for Christian leaders who discount the need to take time-consuming efforts such as confronting an offender privately, then with another brother, when they feel a public official or widely known leader has violated the trust of a large number of people.

"Action must be taken!" they declare. "Such action must be taken quickly." Furthermore, they insist, the Bible doesn't really require that a believer confront a public troublemaker privately first, then with another Christian, then before the church. Such rules are only for problems between individual Christians, today's accusers say.

I disagree. I also say that studying a problem doesn't mean that we are listening to an evil report, either. If the youth director of your church believes that the associate pastor's daughter is stealing her Sunday school class offering, his investigating the problem is not evil. Accused, accuser and any evidence must be examined before any charges are made public. Furthermore, the offender must have a chance to hear the accusation in private — and to repent of it. Obviously, not all suspicions result in proof of guilt. Sometimes the accused is quite innocent.

In cases of guilt followed by sincere, private repentance, leaders must protect the flock by exercising wisdom. We are obligated also to look to man's laws, which would say that if we allow a repentant sex offender to deal with children, a sorrowful embezzler to serve as church treasurer, or a forgiven, court-suspended driver to drive the senior citizens' van, we become negligent and are liable — responsible — for damage that might result.

If you or I have a negative report — are we to bring it before other believers? Yes, but only after we have obeyed Jesus' guidelines first — which often will eliminate the need of having to go public, shouting a brother's sin from the housetops.

Or lamenting a nation's great sin — as did Jeremiah.

Be righteously angry, but do not sin

Jeremiah's heart was broken because of the corruption he saw in those who were called to lead God's people. The self-centeredness and blatant sin among the ministers of his day so crushed him that he trembled like a drunk. He cried:

> *"My heart is broken for the false prophets, full of deceit. ... And the priests are like the prophets, all ungodly, wicked men. I have seen their despicable acts right here in my own Temple, says the Lord." (Jeremiah 23:9, 11).*

While enemy armies were approaching their very gates, "... I have seen in the prophets of Jerusalem a horrible thing: they commit adultery and walk in lies ..." he cried. Preachers were caught in sex sin — then publicly blamed it on others. The Lord suffered ridicule from nonbelievers.

Converts were caught in doubt and disillusionment. Gossip mongers delighted as the scandal grew in naughty detail.

> *"... They encourage and compliment those who are doing evil, instead of turning them back from their sins." (Jeremiah 23:14a).*

Did Jeremiah preach patience and forgiveness of such evil spiritual leaders? Read for yourself:

> *"These prophets are as thoroughly depraved as the men of Sodom and Gomorrah were ... For it is because of them that wickedness fills this land ..." (Jeremiah 23:14b, 15).*

So, is this a license for righteous anger? Once, I held onto enormous anger against a Christian brother whom I believed had purposely hurt my ministry through what I felt was misuse of our funds. I was severely embarrassed. I could not face my supporters with the truth that my outreach had been forced into heavy debt — without my approval.

I wept. I retreated into depression. I contemplated legal charges. I cried before the Lord against this injustice. I refused to forgive. Was I justified? *No.*

What did I do about the brother who wronged me? I almost waited too long. I wallowed in deepening depression for almost two years — pleading that God would step in and resolve my dilemma. Instead, the Lord showed me that I had to forgive and put my mind on things of life — not death.

What happened when I obeyed and gave up the bitterness I harbored? What happened when I put my eyes on Jesus — instead of on the failures of men?

God in His miraculous way repaired our finances. Today, we owe no money to anybody. He restored my peace of mind. I learned that I am not the only Christian who has trouble keeping his eyes on Jesus—and not men. People constantly ask me to pray for their personal healing, or restoration amid crisis, or for protection against Satan in their lives.

Instead of praying immediately, I have learned to inquire whether they are harboring unforgiveness. It is amazing what ugliness surfaces. I know now that to pray for healing for someone who has refused to forgive is virtually useless. Unforgiveness has allowed Satan an entrance into their lives and usually is jeopardizing everything they love—family relationships, careers, ministry, and physical and mental health. Forgiveness must be unconditional. Then God will be faithful to you in your hurts and needs. He will provide healing.

Will He mete out justice? *That's not our problem.* You're not the judge. Nor am I. Only God can judge impartially.

He has promised to raise up in the last days shepherds with the heart and characteristics of David: repentant, God-fearing and jealous for His holiness. If you look around, God has true shepherds. They are few in number and mostly unknown. They do not compromise. They care enough about the flock to call it to repentance. To practice what they preach.

And to rise above the seductive fame, acclaim, applause and adoration of men.

Fame. Acclaim.
Applause. Adoration.

The late John Belushi was one of the legendary stars of the early *Saturday Night Live* TV show. He was a madcap comic with a deadpan craziness. He skyrocketed to fame as a wild *samurai* warrior, a laid-back member of the "Blues Brothers," a glazed-eyed fry cook, a belching fraternity brother and a variety of other ribald characters that caught the imagination of America's young adults.

But it all came to a sudden halt one night when his comic genius was extinguished by cocaine. His life had become a nonstop, party-labeled, narcotic fog as he surrounded himself with people who would not tell him when to quit. This time, he just didn't wake up.

It's not as if we haven't heard this story before, though.

Basketball great Len Bias collapsed and died after a friend persuaded him to give coke a try. The "King of Rock'n'Roll," Elvis Presley, took a decade to destroy himself as he took a wide variety of drugs to wake up, go to sleep, get mellow, get hyper or just try to feel normal.

All three drug deaths stunned the world — although so many entertainers had gone before them — Janis Joplin, Jim Morrison, Johnny Rotten, Lenny Bruce, Diane Linkletter, David Kennedy and Jimi Hendrix to name a few. None of these people were street junkies. And Belushi's sudden drug death was by no means the most tragic or significant.

But his absence was immediately felt by millions of weekly *Saturday Night Live* viewers. There he hadn't just sung or told funny jokes. He'd careened across the set — an enormous, captivating ox of a guy who was gentle, vicious, friendly and terrifying all at once. His yell "Toga party!" echoed across American college campuses — a rebellious call to hedonism. At such parties, the popular drink of the season was the "Purple Jesus" — pure grain alcohol and grape juice. It supposedly got its name from the curse one was supposed to gasp after "chugging" a glass of the breathtaking mixture. Belushi's fans followed his example of "party 'til you drop."

Some died.

The drink faded from popularity partly because of its too-quick effects and partly due to the rash of young collegians suffering from alcohol poisoning — becoming intoxicated so quickly that their bodies lapsed into comas and their brains simply forgot to order the lungs to breathe.

What were John Belushi's fans following? A drug abuser whose sudden wealth and popularity allowed him to do or buy anything his lusts demanded.

Belushi wanted desperately to reach the top of his world. When he made it, he didn't know what to do. As his *Saturday Night Live* success propelled him onto magazine covers and into movie stardom, a great personal emptiness brought him crashing down.

What was his corrupter? Drugs? Alcohol? Sex?

No, it was that same temptation that perhaps gnaws at you as a potentially great Christian leader and teacher.

The approval of men. *Applause.*

Cheers. Adoration. Worship.

Superstardom. Power. Praise. Fame. But mostly *applause.*

You can spend your whole life searching for it. Like Lucifer, you can sacrifice everything in your desperation to achieve it.

A preacher in the Midwest also got caught up in the cheers, the adoration and the worship by TV's millions. In his rather large denomination, he was considered the golden boy.

The angry young man.

The bright and shining hope.

But something went wrong. He disappeared from view. Then, I got some literature from him. On the back of his newsletter he smiled with his arm around a new wife. There was no mention of his singing teenage daughter, whom I heard had left the Lord.

The newsletter was filled with his shocking claims that

American shampoo companies are using the ground-up bodies of aborted babies to get collagen. It was a grisly report. *Disgusting.* I was repulsed at the thought that I might be washing my hair each morning with something made of murdered infants.

Well, I did a little checking. Guess what? The reports are grossly exaggerated, if not blatantly false. They've been around for almost ten years, surfacing in enormous headlines as some publicity hound declares he or she has unearthed new, shocking, shocking news. Apparently, there was an attempt in Europe to put fetuses to such a use, but U.S. health laws blocked it here.

So, here was a formerly prominent evangelist attempting to raise money for his faltering ministry with half truths. "EMERGENCY!" screamed a computer-printed note accompanying the newsletter. "SAVE THE BABIES! WE NEED $1 MILLION TO CARRY ON OUR LONELY BATTLE FOR THE INNOCENTS. Dear Partner: Won't you make this small sacrifice to save just one life? What would Jesus do?"

My stomach was turned. The evangelist was going to use the money to pay his television bills. On TV, he would decry this supposed tragedy — thus justifying his claim that the contribution was helping him to continue his "lonely battle."

Deceiving God's people — even for such a good cause as keeping a ministry on the air — is a symptom of corruption at the worst.

Why do such men desperately struggle to remain on stage? If their support has dried up to such an extent that they have to use outrageous emotional appeals and wild stunts to keep the money rolling in, then is it not time for them to examine their hearts and evaluate their ministries? Is it just a career?

Is it diverting contributions from legitimate TV evangelism just so this evangelist can feed his or her own lust for success? Have he or she taken their eyes off Jesus as they seek the applause? The worship of millions?

Ah, the seductive power of public adoration — and the deception that it breeds. Who pays for secular TV? You and I certainly don't. Everything except the cable channels is absolutely free. *So, who foots the bill for all this free entertainment piped into our homes?*

Advertisers, of course.

And what are they paying for when they pay their thousands to station owners?

Good programs?

Listen, they could care less about good programs.

Advertisers are buying an audience. They are paying the highest dollar for the biggest audiences.

They are buying you and me.

Thus, TV stations have immense financial incentives to put anything on the air that will draw your and my attention. Will a wholesome show about the spiritual yearning of a Bible college student draw millions of viewers?

No.

What will? Sleaze. Violence. Sex. Action. Defiance of authority. Glorification of evil. Darkness. Witchcraft. Murder.

Remember *Miami Vice* when it was brand new? It barely had any plot. It was basically a fast-moving, 60-minute rock video filled with beautiful people, breath-taking shoot-outs, thrilling car and boat chases— and lots of drugs and throbbing music. Millions tuned in. Commercial time went for hundreds of thousands of dollars.

Next in popularity was the sex, sleaze and sneering immorality of *Moonlighting.* Again, it cost a fortune to advertise in that time slot. Why? Because half of America was watching. Meanwhile a 60-second ad could be had for as little as $250 on an independent station showing *Lassie* reruns.

Why? Because no one was watching! You would be throwing your money away since nobody was out there to respond to your advertisement.

Today, wolves come to destroy dressed as angels of light. But they don't have to hide or sneak in nor go door to door. Instead, they are welcomed into our homes and given a place of honor in our living rooms as we hang on every word they say.

On Christian TV, I am particularly disturbed by a number of shows that seem to delight in inviting in the most controversial and extremist spokesmen with some of the most questionable teachings. As dissention, confusion and discouragement spread, the Christian hosts smile and say that they are not responsible for any opinions expressed by their guest today.

Wrong! To not take a stand against evil is sin. Another disturbing thing I see is the growing need for things of God to be entertaining.

No! We must yearn after our Lord, not be trained to sit back and be thrilled. After all, the Gospel is not a magic show.

No more Christian magic shows

Simon the sorcerer in the early Church tried to mix our Lord's supernatural with his own brand of entertainment to fake the anointing that he saw in the disciples. If you remember, Peter rebuked him strongly.

Today, how often do you hear friends talking about how they're going to travel 100 miles to Rev. So-and-So's big crusade so they can see the sick healed? I remember a group of women recently returning from an enormous gathering in New Orleans where they proclaimed having seen a woman raised from the dead.

"I'm going back next year, that's for sure," exclaimed one woman.

Recently, I saw a magazine ad promoting a big convention.

"Signs and Wonders Nightly!" proclaimed the headline. Below was information on how I could attend for only $139 — hotel room not included — and "See God's Miracles!"

Now, wait just a minute. We're selling tickets to see God perform? What if He is offended by this prostitution and decides to demonstrate His great sovereignty with absolute silence? Does everybody get their money back?

What if there are only small miracles? Does everybody get a partial refund? I say this in jest, but my point is very serious. The day of the Christian superstar is fading. What we need today is to get back to the ways of the Book of Acts. The Lord is calling us to holiness. **Holiness.**

A word of caution: This call to holiness is not a call to legalism. It is not a call to observe more laws, rules and regulations. A call to holiness is a call to intimacy with God. To de-

velop a love affair with the Creator of All That Is — romanc
ing Him as He romances us, caring for Him as He cares for
us. To approach His Person with complete transparency,
openly disclosing who we truly are in a humble adoration of
Him. Holiness is not something we can acquire through human efforts.

In the words of my pastor, Don Steiger, the fruit of holiness
is obedience. Holiness is a gift of God!

Once upon a time, another pastor found himself in an
awkward situation. His church needed a new piano player for
the Sunday morning worship.

It was a medium-sized church with enthusiastic praise and
worship, and a song leader who was spontaneous — and required a dedicated accompanist who could keep up with him.

But there was no one in the congregation who could handle
the task. Several teens tried out, but they either could play
beautiful classics, or only by ear — but nothing in between.
And none had been trained to keep up with a director who
was being led of the Spirit.

Finally, the pastor found a candidate — a fine young lady
from a considerably more liberal church down the street. Her
pastor had recommended her — particularly because of her
sweet spirit and willingness to follow the Lord.

So the church's music committee was assembled that Sunday afternoon. Indeed, the pianist was young, attractive and
talented. More than that, she loved Jesus with all her heart.

And she played beautifully. The pastor thanked her and
asked her to wait in his office while the committee made its
decision.

The committee was made up of the song leader, the choir
director, the president of the ladies group and the chairman of
the board of deacons. All were silent for a few moments. Then,
"Congratulations, pastor," said the choir director. "I think
you've got a winner."

"I think she has a little to learn about our style of worship,"
said the song leader. He shrugged agreeably. "However, I
think she'll pick it up very quickly and naturally."

The pastor turned to the president of the women's group,
whom we'll call Edna. Her face was unexpectedly dark with
indignation.

"Honestly, Pastor," she wheezed. "I am shocked."

The pastor took a surprised step backward.

"I'm hurt that you would have suggested that woman at all," exclaimed Edna, her voice growing full of righteous fury. "She's wearing one of those cutesy, short haircuts. The Bible says a woman's hair ought to be long. It seems to me that someone we are inviting to minister on the platform should not be in flagrant disobedience — particularly when so few of the women in our congregation pay any attention any more to that particular passage anyway!"

The pastor nodded thoughtfully. He tried to remember the Bible passage, but could not. It seemed that it was in First or Second Thessalonians. The song leader cleared his throat. It was obvious he was going to say something that they would all regret.

"Ah," interrupted the pastor. "Ah ... Edna, let me see if I understand you correctly." He grinned his most winning pastoral smile. "You feel that her hair is too short to play the piano?"

"That's right," snapped Edna.

"But, Edna," popped off the choir director, "I saw it with my own eyes. She used her hands to play the piano, not her hair."

Even Edna could not help but smile. Later that evening, she gave in and voted for hiring the pianist. *Of course, she made a point within the week of meeting with the young lady and discussing hair length ....*

The problem, of course, was not hair. It was holiness — or what people believe holiness to be. Holiness is the distinctive mark and signature of God in our lives. It speaks of the way in which God separates us, calls us out to be His servants. But it can't be perceived with our eyes alone.

Holiness is not tears. Neither is it long hair on a woman. Nor, as we learned in the 1970s, is it short hair on a man.

Since we are merely human, we'll never achieve the perfection that Jesus demonstrated. But God will strengthen us to press toward holiness in obedience. We just have to call on Him.

Look what happens to our society and our church when we don't! As I view our society — which disdains such solutions and scoffs at the idea of a God who is protecting, providing, teaching, guiding us constantly — I am filled with anguish.

Just look where it is going without Him! *We have lost our fear of God!* Fear of God? Is that important? It certainly is. By fear, I mean respect.

Reverence.

Obedience because we don't want to suffer the frustrations of a life without His blessings.

Get out your Bible and check out these Scriptures:

- *Proverbs 10:27 — A healthy fear of God will lengthen your life.*
- *Proverbs 15:16 — Fear of the Lord brings contentment.*
- *Proverbs 16:6 — Fear of the Lord helps us overcome sinful habits.*
- *Proverbs 22:4 — Fear of the Lord results in riches and honor!*
- *Psalm 5:7 — Fear of the Lord will give you freedom in praising and worshiping Him.*
- *Psalm 25:14 — The person who fears God will be given the secrets of the Lord.*
- *Psalm 34:7-10 — God's protection is with those who fear Him*
- *Psalm 60:4 — Truth will be evident in the life of those who fear the Lord.*
- *Psalm 103:13 — Those who fear the Lord will have His mercy.*
- *Psalm 147:11 — The Lord takes pleasure in those who fear Him.*

What happens without fear of the Lord? A society run amock — with everybody doing whatever seems right in their own eyes. That's what we're living in these days. And what is it producing?

I read a book review in a secular newspaper that told of a "wonderful" best-seller with sex that dripped from nearly every page. The critic called this author's first novel a "candy box of vulgarity." Filled with sex perversion, drinking, and drug addiction, the book was destined to become a blockbuster movie, he forecasted.

Brothers and sisters, what is happening to us? Sure enough, that's exactly what happened to that book! Later I read in a news magazine as an editor told of being invited to watch the filming of the movie version. She said about her visit to the movie set, "I heard more four-letter words in ten days on that set than I heard in four years at [college]."

That's what happens when a world gone crazy no longer presses forward toward purity. The darkness of the human heart allows us to sink backward into the mire and death of the world. Another best-seller was touted for its stunning realism as it told the shocking story of homosexuality and drug use among youngsters of Southern California. What possible good can such a book do?

It makes money — millions of dollars for the author, the publisher and the distributors. Sure, it may shatter thousands of lives and lead innocent, lonely kids into death and despair. But the people who produce such "blockbusters" don't worry about that. They're too busy counting their millions. If accused, they will pull out secular psychologist's studies that claim that we are unaffected by what we read. I shudder at such selfishness.

How can someone not care about the damage that such a book does to tender minds and hearts? How can riches make up for it? In their desperate climb to be number one, authors, magazine editors, movie producers, and television executives prostitute themselves to seek new and more exciting ways to portray decadence, sex and violence.

One book's ads claimed it described more than a thousand seductions. Another advised young women on how to trap married men. Other books are billed as sex-filled, sadistic and orgiastic. A reviewer said in recommending one novel, "Color this one dirty. It's been a while since I've seen so much filth outside the barnyard." *That's good?*

Yes, if you don't believe in the journey toward holiness, it can seem good. So, how do we fight back?

Holiness.

A yearning for the mind of Christ. A love from Jesus that is unpretentious, sincere and down-to-earth.

If you stick to that, you'll find yourself growing increasingly immune to the deceits of the world, the flesh and the devil. You'll find yourself wanting to win the world and keeping your eyes on Jesus. Once you begin to achieve this, are you qualified to become a modern-day Pharisee, establishing rules and regulations for young believers, ordaining for them what is good, what is not very good, what is forbidden and what will send them straight to hell?

Of course not.

Then, how do we remedy this terrible state of affairs? Through personal holiness. Through your and my seeking our Lord and striving to be like Him. How? How can we do this in our perverse society?

• Through daily prayer — a quiet time with the Lord at dawn. You'll be astonished at its effect on your life.

• Through dedicated Bible reading. Get an understandable translation. Although it's not the best for deep Bible study, Tyndale House's *The Living Bible* paraphrase is excellent for first-time daily Bible readers. And one of the very best daily Bible-reading plans, *The Victory Bible Reading Plan,* is produced by Jim McKeever's Omega Publications out in Medford, Oregon. If reading the whole Bible boggles you, try an incredibly valuable little booklet put out by Regal Books called *The Jesus Person Pocket Promise Book* by Dave Wilkerson.

• Through fellowship with solid believers. You'd best pray about this one. If you're not growing in the Lord with the Christians with whom you worship and socialize, begin taking this problem before the Lord.

God has shown us a different way to heaven. It's not by "being good enough" and trying to obey each of God's rules for living. Paul in Romans 3:21,22 proclaims "God says he will accept and acquit us — declare us 'not guilty' — if we trust Jesus Christ to take away our sins."

If we are saved by faith, does this mean we no longer need to obey God's laws? Just the opposite, he writes in chapter 8:9:

> *"You are controlled by your new nature if you have the Spirit of God living in you."*

Do we really know what it means to seek holiness? That is the question I ask myself when reading about past revivals. What will it take for Christians today to desire holiness as our forebears did?

Is holiness for now or for yesterday? Often we are too busy

praying for material provisions and are not aware of the importance of holiness in our lives. There are those who wrongly believe that holiness went out with the Puritans and Queen Victoria. Others feel that holiness was only for prophets and monks — men such as Elijah and St. John of the Cross.

Still others laugh at the idea of holiness as something we've outgrown — something that you find up in the Ozarks or the Tennessee hills with primitive, unlearned folk who wear black shawls and sing "Do Lord."

Holiness used to be difficult for me to understand, too.

This is partly because we Christians often are more concerned with what others demand of us rather than what our Lord Jesus Christ expects of us.

I believe holiness is for you and me — here and now! The Apostle Paul apparently agreed with me, for here's what he told the Christians in Rome:

> *"But now you are free from the power of sin and are slaves of God, and his benefits to you include holiness and everlasting life" (Rom. 6:22).*

And here's what he said to the church in Ephesus:

> *"Long ago, even before he made the world, God chose us to be his very own, through what Christ would do for us; he decided then to make us holy in his eyes, without a single fault — we who stand before him covered with his love" (Eph. 1:4).*

The skeptic in you is probably protesting: "But, Nicky, though it may be true that we're called to be holy, that won't happen until we get to Heaven. Then we'll be holy and blameless in His sight, but no sooner."

I disagree. So does the author of Hebrews. He writes,

> *"...we have been forgiven and made clean by Christ's dying for us once and for all" (Heb. 10:10).*

Notice the use of the past tense: "...we have been ...."

A few verses later he repeats this thought but adds another insight:

> *"By that one offering he made forever perfect in the sight of God all those whom he is making holy" (Heb. 10:14).*

In other words, holiness is not a mystical state of consciousness that suddenly comes over us like the shivers. Rather, it is a pilgrimage of sorts that undergirds our everyday experiences.

Many Christians get discouraged when they come across Scriptures that relate to holiness. Take the exhortation from Peter:

> *"But be holy now in everything you do, just as the Lord is holy, who invited you to be his child. He himself has said, 'You must be holy, for I am holy'"* (1 Peter 1:15-16).

Typically the reader says to himself, "Sure, Peter, easy for you to say. Aren't you asking me to be like God, to be perfect?"

The answer is NO! To be holy is to be set apart for God's use and pleasure as His treasured possession. It means being on God's wavelength so that communication and fellowship are possible. It means walking in His steps; doing things God's way; and being a vessel for the Holy Spirit.

> *"In a wealthy home there are dishes made of gold and silver as well as some made from wood and clay. The expensive dishes are used for guests, and the cheap ones are used in the kitchen or to put garbage in. If you stay away from sin you will be like one of these dishes made of purest gold—the very best in the house—so that Christ himself can use you for his highest purposes"* (II Tim. 2:20-22).

Are we getting confused with expectations? Be careful not to think of holiness as some spiritual trophy to be won or earned. Holiness cannot be attained by tithing, by good deeds, nor by intellectual knowledge. How, then, can we become holy?

We are more than conquerors

Holiness is a gift from God. I've said that a number of times in this book. But let me say it again. Holiness is a gift from God. Only He can make us holy.

"...I am Jehovah who makes you holy," God instructed Moses in Exodus 31:13. Only the Lord can cleanse our attitudes and motives.

Yet, holiness is more than a state of mind and heart. It implies activity, not a passive life of sitting around being nice and sweet and good.

Holiness produces a willingness to dig in and do unpleasant tasks, to care for the unlovely and the ungrateful, and to sacrifice one's personal pride and ambitions for the Kingdom.

Beware, too, of thinking of holiness as the badge worn by an exclusive spiritual club with rigid legal restrictions, rituals, standards, grooming requirements and personal ethics.

Outward appearances and performance are not holiness. Remember: truth minus love does not equal holiness.

Holiness is an outgrowth of our relationship with God. The more we give our undivided attention to that relationship, the holier we become.

David's walk with God clearly demonstrates this principle. He was the writer of the beautiful Psalms, which give me daily inspiration and strength. Yet, David was an adulterer and a murderer. Though David often made mistakes and fell into sin, I'm convinced that God found him holy. Why? Because David desired to know God above all other things. He also had a true, repentant heart and humbled himself.

David was a man after God's own heart. He could be counted

on to do everything the Lord wanted him to do. (Acts 13:22) We learn from David, then, that holiness is really a desire for God, and a passion to do what pleases Him. David's Psalms reflect this yearning. In Psalm 63:1, for example, David says,

"O God, my God! How I search for you! How I thirst for you in this parched and weary land where there is no water. How I long to find you!"

But all this doesn't mean that we get to live lives of casual sin, then expect God to declare us holy. Look at what the Lord told Israel in Deuteronomy 28:9:

"He will change you into a holy people dedicated to himself; this he has promised to do if you will only obey him and walk in his ways."

Holiness is grounded on commitment, not feelings. David's words are charged with emotion. Yet, we must be careful not to confuse holiness with depth of emotion. Holiness is grounded on commitment, not feelings.

What is commitment?

When we choose to be holy, we choose to offer ourselves as living sacrifices. We are to be holy and acceptable to God.

"And so, dear brothers, I plead with you to give your bodies to God. Let them be a living sacrifice, holy — the kind he can accept. When you think of what he has done for you, is this too much to ask? Don't copy the behavior and customs of this world, but be a new and different person with a fresh newness in all you do and think. Then you will learn from your own experience how his ways will really satisfy you" (Rom. 12:1-2) /

We stand ready to review our ambitions, preconceptions and expectations.

We begin to seek God's best, not our own.

We accept the possibility that our rewards may not come in the form of success on the job, financial windfall or poolside vacations.

Finally, we give up our independence and admit that without God, we are nothing and can do nothing. That would seem a good enough reason to be holy, but here's one more reason:

"Try to stay out of all quarrels and seek to live a clean and holy life, for one who is not holy will not see the Lord" (Heb. 12:14).

I don't know about you, but I want to see the Lord. I want to spend eternity with Him. That's reason enough for me to seek His holiness in my life.

We need to wake up and learn from history. We have violated God's laws. Just as our forefathers needed to fall on their faces in repentant sorrow, we must come before the Lord in brokenness, willing to sacrifice all. We must love one another — ignoring denominational barriers. We must require humility of our spiritual leaders and shun the superstar mentality that has brought us such terrible disgrace in recent months.

We must bring back the fear of the Lord!

How to hear
the Lord's voice

If we want to be holy, we must spend time with the Holy One. We cannot attain holiness through our own efforts or through our own strengths or actions. As we intimately relate to our Heavenly Father and spend our time with Him, His character is infused in us and we become like Him as we are influenced by His holy presence. Most of the teaching we hear today about holiness requires us to follow a rule, law or "biblical principle."

Many teachers tell us the way to holiness is to first obey God. Others teach us if you want to be holy, you must trust God. Yet, others impose rules and regulations to acquire holiness.

But how can you obey someone you don't know? How can you trust someone who has not proven their love for you? It is impossible to be holy unless we surrender our heart and mind to a total, intimate relationship with our Lord. Intimacy with the Lord is a glorious thing.

How do we hear? Consider this divinely inspired advice Paul offered his young co-worker, Timothy:

> *"Work hard so God can say to you 'Well done.' Be a good workman, one who does not need to be ashamed when God examines your work. Know what his Word says and means. Steer clear of foolish discussions which lead people into the sin of anger with each other" (II Tim. 2:15-18).*

Do you understand that last part? First, Paul told Timothy to study the Scriptures diligently. Then he offered an example of human doctrine — that the Second Coming had already occurred and the Church had missed it.

This human foolishness was causing believers to stumble. So, how was young Timothy supposed to tell the difference between God's wisdom and human foolishness?

Here is how Paul advised the Church in Philippi:

> *"Always be full of joy in the Lord; I say it again, rejoice! Let everyone see that you are unselfish and considerate in all you do. Remember that the Lord is coming soon. Don't worry about anything; instead, pray about everything; tell God your needs and don't forget to thank him for his answers. If you do this you will experience God's peace, which is far more wonderful than the human mind can understand. His peace will keep your thoughts and your hearts quiet and at rest as you trust in Christ Jesus"* (Phil. 4:4-9).

But, how do we hear God's voice? How, as we study the Word do we know God's will — as opposed to our own imagination — as we desire with all our hearts to to get a personal revelation from the Almighty? Here's what the author of the Book of Hebrews advised:

> *"Since we have such a huge crowd of men of faith watching us from the grandstands, let us strip off anything that slows us down or holds us back, and especially those sins that wrap themselves so tightly around our feet and trip us up; and let us run with patience the particular race that God has set before us"* (Heb. 12:1-2).

The Apostle Peter adds:

> *"So now you can look forward soberly and intelligently to more of God's kindness to you when Jesus Christ returns. Obey God because you are his children; don't slip back into your old ways — doing evil because you knew no better. But be holy now in everything you do, just as the Lord is holy, who invited you to be his child"* (I Pet. 1:13-16).

Faith and obedience walk hand in hand. If you're having trouble obeying, faith may be lacking. But it's good to know that faith comes from hearing the Word of God.

James agrees:

> *"So get rid of all that is wrong in your life, both inside and outside, and humbly be glad for the wonderful message we have received, for it is able to save our souls as it takes hold of our hearts." (James 1:21-22).*

Listening to the Lord is not a clever technique teachable in one easy lesson. It is a lifestyle of obedience.

Only as a holy people can we wait upon the Lord and recognize His still, small voice of divine guidance—and rightly discern if it is He ... or the evil one ... or our own impatient, desperate desire to hear *something.*

One night, many years ago during the beginning stages of my ministry, I was in prayer. I was in a very run-down motel and my quarters consisted of just a bed in a very small room. Here in this room, I had one of the most significant experiences of my life. As I began to pray and seek God, something extraordinary happened to me. I began to sense a great intimacy with God. A closeness that transcended all physical presence. I felt caught up in the very presence of my Heavenly Father. It was a closeness, an intimacy in which no secrets existed. I began to weep, breaking down before God as I recognized His mighty presence in an awesome way.

I recognized I was nothing and that He was everything. I recognized my total dependency on Him. With rivers of tears flooding down my face and a loud sobbing, I told Him I loved Him, that He was my Lord, my King, my Strength, my Power, and that without Him, I was nothing. God recognized my worthlessness and yet in His passionate love for me, He touched me and invested all of Himself to make me an effective child — to make me what He wanted me to be.

I was with Him in an intimate way. *He touched **me.***

And as He touched me, I changed.

That day, I discovered the true secret of how to become what God wanted me to become. The secret was not to fast more, to read the Bible more, to go to church more or to get more formal education. No, the secret was intimacy with my God. Because of this closeness, a genuine desire swells up within me to read the Bible, to fast, to go to church and to become the person God wants me to be. *And that is holiness.*

At the time of my experience, I was struggling to understand what God had done in my life.

I was undermining my own conversion experience and God's miracle in my life. This was a time in which God was molding me and changing me. I was very tender before Him, allowing Him to shape my will.

I was facing many conflicts and pressures in Bible school and trying to live up to many different expectations of Christians all around me.

At this time, I began to recognize God's greatness and His unfailing love for me that went beyond words and experience. I began to have a deep burden for the lost, including my father and family who were deeply involved in witchcraft. I knew something great was happening to me.

After that experience, I was like a young puppy wanting and yearning more and more to be in the arms of my Master. Being in the intimate presence of God is to have a sweet, sweet feeling of peace and tranquility that, as the Bible says "passes all understanding." It is too powerful to articulate. It must be experienced.

I was taken into the highest places with God in the Spirit as He revealed Himself to me for about seven hours as I was bathed in His love and mercy.

Afterward, I could not walk and did not feel like eating. My body hurt and my bones were aching. But my spirit was soaring.

God had cared enough about worthless ol' me to lift me into heavenly aeries where I understood for the first time His goodness, power, love, protection and kindness.

I was 19 years old, but the experience was the beginning of my new romance with God. I became so deeply *enamorado* — in love — with Him that I had no more doubts of His love and faithfulness and deep commitment to me. Was this a one-time experience? No!

I was invited to preach in a desperately poor country tucked into a humid corner of the world. It is a country under terrible spiritual and political oppression. Once before, I had encountered intense opposition there from native shamans — witch doctors and sorcerers — who did not like my message at all nor the fact that our crusade was filling the largest stadiums in the country. But this time, as I entered the country, I felt a great closeness to and protection of the Most High. I enjoyed a particularly powerful anointing. God would speak to me tenderly and so lovingly — guiding me in what I should say. Again, I felt caught up to heavenly places. I was nourished, nurtured and strengthened in my spirit. It was clean, pure — and I wanted more of it! This was a reminder of that love affair in my heart with my Lord. I was still reminded that He had not changed, even though the world around me has. I sensed the reassurance that He completely guides, directs me and that He will never let me down.

I felt lost as the dark clouds moved in and approached the staduim packed with 45,000 people. As I stood there, I felt like a little ant, totally helpless and insignificant. I felt depressed and troubled as darkness filled the entire stadium for a few minutes. The mighty umbrella of a powerful darkness of the devil moved into the arena to intimidate us. There was a force of 2,000 witches behind this entire orchestration, but the Lord moved in, breaking through in a powerful way while I was gasping for air and a solution.

Through the power of praying Christians, hell was destroyed in a supernatural way and people just fell in love with Jesus. The realization hit me that I could not defend myself, that I had no strategy worth putting forward. It was God's and only God's divine strategy straight from heaven that was powerful and capable enough to conquer this attack.

Again I felt the intense heartbeat of the Gospel of evangelism. I was inspired as I saw again how God reaches out to touch all needy people in a personal way.

So, I say to you that if you want to hear the Lord, if you are having trouble obeying, trusting Him or feeling holy, then open yourself to the Lord and desire an intimacy with Him. Pray for just that! Get away from distractions, fast for a couple of days and just seek the Almighty Lord. You will find Him to be right where He has always been. Beside you. *Caring about you.* Loving you.

I believe that this intimacy one-on-one with God is the true key to restoring our Church. Being with Him is our only hope for change, for He is the only One that can change the heart of man.

"But Nicky," you may protest, "by teaching us to expect to hear God, you're producing more of the false prophets so rampant among us these days!"

Well, do foolish people who falsely claim to speak for God prove that no one hears from Him any more? No! In fact, the Bible prophesies that false prophets will come in the last days — and teaches us how to deal with their false messages! *Should we reject Jesus just because false messiahs appeared in His day? No!* Satan produced those bogus christs to confuse those watching for His coming. And that's the role of false prophets today. To discredit our Heavenly Father's true spokesmen. Thus, it's up to us to test the word of any prophet against God's Word:

> "Do not smother the Holy Spirit. Do not scoff at those who prophesy, but test everything that is said to be sure it is true ..." (I Thessalonians 5:19-21).

If someone introduces into your fellowship some grand new idea, search the Scriptures. Is there biblical precedence for corporate dancing? How about the giving or naming of spiritual gifts? Chanting? Miraculous tooth-filling or leg-lengthening? Creative confession? The deification of man — that we are all destined to become little gods? Classes in how to prophesy or speak in tongues? Memory healing? Interpretation of dreams?

Did they do it in the early Church? Did they teach against it? Listen: our brotherhood is severely divided these days over some of the things I've just listed. It doesn't matter how I feel about any of them. What does the Bible say?

Are you qualified to search the Scriptures about these devisive problems? Of course! Are you permitted to ask the Lord to speak to your heart about any of these things?

Absolutely!

But be *so careful* about declaring you have been given a divine word. The devil molds such convincing counterfeits. Recently a young would-be author was telling how *the Lord had assured her abortion is acceptable in His sight!*

What a horrible lie!

"It just felt so good to know I had not murdered my baby," she said. "Instead, I knew aborted children go straight to heaven and skip life's hassles."

What a terrible twisting of reality! Sure, murdered babies avoid earth's trials—but that gives us no right to kill them! Here was a woman so filled with guilt over destroying the life of her unborn child that she had accepted a beautiful, "divine revelation" — which was false, demonic and destructive! She did not consider her "word" in light of the Bible. Why was that a mistake?

> *"The whole Bible was given to us by inspiration from God and is useful to teach us what is true and to make us realize what is wrong in our lives; it straightens out and helps us do what is right" (II Timothy 3:16).*

Great men of God such as David occasionally heard the word of the Lord through prophets. But notice what the adulterous David did when the prophet Nathan brought God's word of judgment and the news that David's newborn son would die:

> *"Then Nathan returned to his home. And the Lord made Bath-sheba's baby deathly sick. David begged him to spare the child, and went without food and lay all night before the Lord on the bare earth." (II Samuel 12:15-16)*

David did not ask Nathan to pray for him or the baby. David went before the Lord in repentance and great sorrow. He also was awaiting a sign from the Lord. It came in action instead of words when the baby died:

> *"Then, on the seventh day, the baby died. David's aides were afraid to tell him.*
>
> *" 'He was so broken up about the baby being sick,' they said, 'what will he do to himself when we tell him the child is dead?'*
>
> *"But when David saw them whispering, he realized what had happened.*
>
> *" 'Is the baby dead?' he asked.*
>
> *" 'Yes,' they replied, 'he is.' Then David got up off the ground, washed himself, brushed his hair, changed his clothes, and went into the Tabernacle and worshiped the Lord. Then he returned to the palace and ate. His aides were amazed. 'We don't understand you,' they told him. 'While the baby was still living, you wept and refused to eat; but now that the baby is dead, you have stopped your mourning and are eating again.'*

> *"David replied, 'I fasted and wept while the child was
> alive, for I said, "Perhaps the Lord will be gracious to me
> and let the child live." But why should I fast when he is
> dead? Can I bring him back again? I shall go to him, but he
> shall not return to me '" (II Sam. 12:18-23).*

David recognized that Nathan's word for him was indeed from
the Lord. But he took it from there — one-on-one with his
Creator.

Rejoice if those you know and trust believe that they hear
Him telling them things about you. But don't accept it blindly.

Take it before the Lord.

Your faith is in the Lord alone, not men — no matter how
righteous they appear. Never step aside and let others take your
place before the throne of the Most High.

Be wary of rationalizations by people who cite their spiritual
credentials and assure you they know more about God's will
than common folk such as you and I. Certainly, you need to sit
under qualified teachers, but you owe it to them to investigate
everything they teach you. You will benefit if you fill your life
with the wisdom shared by God's great human writers and
speakers. But test everything against the Word and in prayer
during your daily quiet time with the Lord.

When you quit communing with the Most High and are
content to let somebody else "hear God" for you, the life-giving
link between you and your Father is cut. If your leaders—those
you are trusting to hear for you—take their eyes off of Jesus and
begin attempting His work in their own human strengths and
wisdom, you will find yourself adrift from the Almighty God.

Too many times the trusting followers don't notice that their
human shepherd has strayed. Obediently they follow him down
dead-end trails.

Futility results. Wasted effort.

Wasted emotion.

Wasted money.

Wasted years. Be so, so cautious of prayer meetings that almost turn into seances as visiting "prophets" pray over each person and foretell coming events.

"Christian humanism" creeps in so subtly where human
authority is stressed, so gradually that no docile, trusting sheep

dares to raise concerns that their "great man of God" has become self-directed and out of God's will.

A cult leader will trap his prey in a snare of deception and control. He tells his followers that he knows what is best for them and that they should not question his authority. Hundreds followed Jim Jones into the jungles of Guyana where on his command they participated in the vilest of sexual deviance, then committed suicide *en masse* — to the horror of the watching world.

Charles Manson convinced his murdering followers that he alone knew what was best for them.

We have seen groups such as Fundamentalists Anonymous get publicity providing "support groups" for people who leave churches that try to dominate their lives and for "deprogramming" Christians caught up in fellowships that exercise excessive control.

A number of recent court cases have forced evangelists to return large sums of money to contributors whose families claimed they were "brainwashed" into donating millions. Satan would like to see the Church branded as one more dangerous cult.

He has succeeded in the Soviet Union.

Let's not help him do it here.

Let us guard our hearts against the desire to control other Christians' lives. We do not know what is best for them. That's a matter between them and their Maker. Our job is to get the two in touch.

The late David du Plessis once declared that God has no grandchildren. *That's still true*. You cannot get into Heaven because your parents are holy. I cannot come into His Presence through the intercession of anyone but Jesus Christ.

Each of us must come to the Father on our own. We must have our own personal relationship with Him.

One-on-one.

You and the Creator of All That Is.

Me and the mighty Master of the Universe.

We each must examine our hearts. Although we continue to use Christian terminology and declare ourselves believers ... if our faith is in human wisdom and if our hearts belong to someone or something else than our Lord and Savior, then our fruits will be empty and worthless — although they may look nice from afar. We will sound the wrong alarms. We will denounce those who should not be denounced. And our churches will become whitewashed sepulchres where people gather to bicker and fight over doctrinal motes. They will become landscaped garbage dumps where the rag-pickers judge each other loudly to heaven above.

And eventually they will become cold, empty cathedrals admired only by gawking tourists.

The biggest church in America

You may think you recognize the participants in this next story. But let me explain that it is a composite — a retelling of numerous actual events that as I write this are occurring on both coasts of the United States.

There was a pastor who desired to have the biggest church building in America. He labored before the Lord, baring his soul and repeating his desire to preach to thousands each Sunday. To make an enormous impact on the community. To erect a beacon of hope and a temple of righteousness for the ungodly to see — a testimony of God's greatness.

One Sunday, he took it before his 7,000 member congregation at all four morning services. The paid orchestra stirred hearts during the multi-media presentation outlining the mission ahead.

During the pastor's beautifully delivered, emotionally charged sermon, "A Declaration of War on the Devil," his 15-member ministry staff stood applauding behind him on the platform. At the end of each of the services, the pastor's 10 elders joined him at the pulpit as he — with musical fanfare and tears from his wife — unveiled the architect's sketch of a 10,000-seat sanctuary.

But there were voices of dissension.

In the second service, an elderly woman stood and proclaimed the "word of the Lord" that God would not bless this plan to take on a $23 million debt. When she stayed for the third service, apparently intending to repeat her "word," the ushers asked her to give up her seat. At that next service, the pastor got his own "word of the Lord" that the building was already theirs — and that it only had to be claimed in faith and by the signing of pledge cards being handed out by the deacons.

Over the next 24 months, the massive structure rose. It was opened amid much publicity. TV crews filmed the faithful rising to the balconies by escalator. Off-duty police directed traffic. A nationally known recording artist appeared at the dedication.

Telegrams of congratulations rolled in from politicians, evangelists, community leaders and national Christian celebrities.

But the board of elders was secretly divided over a number of issues, not the least of which was $19 million in cost over-runs. Some also were disturbed about the parking situation. Others were upset about procedural and administrative matters — particularly dealing with the church's cash flow — and what they saw as political maneuvering by the staff. Three of the young assistant pastors on the ministerial staff quit to start their own churches. One took 1,200 members with him to a local high school auditorium where he began an exciting healing and deliverance ministry.

Offerings back at the original congregation nosedived. Attendance dipped below 3,000. Rumors surfaced that the orchestra leader was having an affair with the ministries administrator's wife and that the director of the church's locally broadcast TV outreach had a prescription drug problem.

Then, the pastor felt he had to remove a highly popular assistant he had brought in to preach on the frequent Sunday mornings when the pastor had to travel to national speaking engagements and meetings of top leadership. The angered assistant promptly started another congregation in a very affluent part of town, taking 400 of the top tithers with him. After the pastor denounced his action from the pulpit the next Sunday morning, the chairman of the elders quit — then sent the following letter, which somehow got into wide circulation. I have redone — and shortened — the letter to avoid identifying or embarrassing anyone.

Dear Pastor:
I was just chatting with with my wife about my plans of having a pleasant breakfast with you next week and

avoiding anything unpleasant. She, however, thought that our breakfast might should be a lay-it-all-on-the-table time.

My immediate responses were:

1) You are much too important a person to be interested in what I might think about your recent performances; 2) I don't care to be the subject of a Sunday sermon about an angry, misguided reprobate who ruined your day; 3) What does it matter? You and I have taken completely separate paths. Your choices and my choices have ordained that we will have little in common. So, what's the point in any ugliness between us?

Let us be friends, saying nice things about each other. Let bygones be bygones. Let us think the best of each other, forgetting what might have been, what we believe should have been ... or who did the other dirt;

But on the other hand, I can't help but wonder if it's time someone stood up and spoke into your life.

I'm not sure. I believe it would have to be shouted from the housetops if you are to pay any attention.

But here goes:

You have used your ability to manipulate facts, sway emotions and set moods to deceive a lot of trusting people. The danger is that when they discover your untruths, they are going to doubt a great deal of their spiritual experience, particularly where it concerns anything you taught them. You frequently lead people to believe that which is not, then can defend yourself by saying that you didn't actually say that which was interpreted — and that you have no control over what people think they hear.

However, you have a great deal of control.

And you use it toward your own ends. One particularly destructive facet of all this is your habit of promising folks power and control and position when you have no intention of carrying through. You cannot be trusted. Your yes is not yes. Your no is not no. In uncomfortable positions, you much rather say one ear-tickling thing to one person and its soothing opposite to someone else. You do not keep confidences. You are frantic to please all men.

You have compromised your integrity by aligning your-self with national religious power centers that are now being discredited. It would have been wiser to trust the Father to lift you up wherever He wanted you to be. Trusting Him, you could have been bold and truthful — whereas the path you took has caused you to see nothing wrong with sin. You've rationalized and closed your eyes when you could have been John the Baptist. On a person-al note, I believe you've been afraid to be bold when deal-ing with actual adultery on your staff. Why don't you stand up on your own two feet? Why do you need to align yourself with such materialism and anxiousness to ap-peal to men?

Well, that's enough.

I'm somewhat uncomfortable in writing this.

I have heard how you write off people who irritate you by speaking bluntly. I've also been warned by at least five people that you are deaf — that there is a spiritual op-pression that has you bound and unable to hear these things, all of which have been said before — and that there is no point in my burning bridges and saying impo-lite things in public. The Lord did not order me to "speak these truths into your life."

I'm hardly perfect. Who am I to be shouting about the splinter in your eye? And where do I get off criticizing a great man of God, a self-proclaimed apostle quoted in the big-city press, an important servant of the Most High?

If you're interested in my recommendation, pray that the Lord will send you your own personal Nathan — the prophet who informed King David of his sin. Pray that you'll recognize him when he comes and that you'll have your strength restored to act on his warnings.

Ah, well. Perhaps you understand why I would much rather just enjoy a pleasant breakfast with an old friend and chat about your congregation's now-$42-million debt or somesuch. But somebody had to speak. I, personally, probably am not the best candidate. I voted with my dusty feet to make all this stuff none of my business. It's much more pleasant to leave it so and worship elsewhere.

But this world is not always a pleasant place.

Your friend ...

Brothers and sisters, step back for a moment and look at how successful the demonic tactics were in this case. Here we have good Christians denouncing and alienating each other — and burning in their anger.

Where is their desire to win the lost? It's forgotten in all the uproar! All this other stuff has gotten in the way. Do you see the corrupter's game plan? *Keep us at each other's throats and we'll be unable to help a dying world.*

It appears to me that somebody charged into battle without legitimate orders from the Commander-in-Chief.

When we attempt to fight God's battles without knowing Him or hearing His orders, we are no more effective than any other army whose infantry is wandering off in any direction it pleases. Like modern-day medieval Crusaders, we go in search of Holy Grails, vowing to kill any infidels defiling whatever we declare to be Holy Land.

We employ logical, human solutions — which seldom are God's solutions.

Today, many Christian alarm-sounders do this very thing, I believe. In their rashness, I believe they rationalize away any need for the Bible's guidelines for accusing the brethren. They discount the need to take time-consuming efforts such as confronting an offender privately, then with another brother, when they feel a public official or widely known leader has violated the trust of a large number of people.

"Action must be taken!" they declare.

Instead, we must **diligently study God's Word** and **wait for our very-much-alive Jesus' guidance** through the Helper He promised — the Holy Spirit.

It is extremely popular to attack *secular humanism* on every side. Yet, we seem blind to the horrible truth that its brother has permeated the Church. *Christian humanism* has inflicted itself on us from the first.

Here's what Paul told Timothy about those who fail to check with the Lord God before announcing His will — in this case concerning ancient law:

> *"... these teachers ... spend their time arguing and talking foolishness. They want to become famous as*

*teachers of the laws of Moses when they haven't the
slightest idea what those laws really show us. Those laws
are good when used as God intended. But they were not
made for us, whom God has saved ..." (I Tim. 1:6-9).*

If you read that whole chapter carefully, you'll realize Paul
wasn't talking about pagans. He was decrying Christian
teachers taking the Gospel off onto all sorts of side roads.
Paul goes on to advise Timothy:

*"But the Holy Spirit tells us clearly that in the last times
some in the church will turn away from Christ and become
eager followers of teachers with devil-inspired ideas. These
teachers will tell lies with straight faces and do it so often
their consciences won't even bother them" (I Tim. 4:1,2).*

What does all this mean? Some men foolishly attempt to
solve God's "problems" for Him out of greed for the tithes of
God's people, some out of lust for power and recognition, and
others purely out of ignorance, not knowing how to seek God or
hear His voice. One example would be a pastor who recently
advised a women to divorce her lazy husband — and gave her
a check from the church treasury for the legal fees. Another example would be denominations which — in the name of human
rights — contribute to atheistic causes such as funding communistic "liberation fronts" in the Third World.

Another would be the visiting prophet who glibly has an exciting prophecy for everybody who comes to him for prayer —
when in fact he is not hearing from the Lord in every case and
is having to rely every now and then on his human wits and
the insights of someone who knows how to make people happy.

I believe we often practice Christian humanism with
good intentions—because we are ignorant of God's Word and
unwilling to stand up against corrupt traditions, human dog-
mas, false interpretations and outright inventions passing
themselves off as Christianity.

It also happens when we attempt to set ourselves up as authorities on God's ways before the Lord has called us to the
task. Unqualified, we shoot off our mouths — talking about
things of which we know much too little. *But don't despair.*
Christian humanism can be cured with each believer falling
on his face before God in repentance and asking for guidance,

grace, wisdom, revelation and strength to obey the Lord's clear instructions.

Bill recently attended a week-long conference lead by a prominent spiritual teacher and his heir-apparent son. In one evening session, the offering was passed eight times as the teacher pleaded for thousands of dollars — and as people in threadbare clothes put their last $5 in the basket.

"Lord," prayed my friend as the teacher began pleading again, "Lord, how can you bless this fraud?"

Trembling in anger, my friend bowed his head as the usher handed him the collection basket again. *"Lord, this teacher is a fake! His appeals are as transparent as a snake-oil peddler's! He's stealing from these sweet, trusting folks!"*

Then, deep inside his heart, there came a sudden realization: *That teacher up there is human, just like you. I love him in the same way that I love you. And I expect you to love him, too, just as you are supposed to love any sinner or any believer. His sin is My business, not yours.*

Bill sat in stunned silence. "Father," he prayed in silence. "Forgive me. Forgive me."

Did he penitently put $100 in the basket?

No, at the end of the service, he left, never to return to any session led by that particular teacher.

But he quit accusing the teacher before the Lord. That's what Satan does. Many of us forget Jesus' very plain instructions to lay aside our concern about that splinter in our brother's eye when, instead, we should seek remedy for the 2-by-4 we're ignoring in our own eye.

That's an interesting comparison that our Lord used. He must have wanted to bring our attention to the fact that being judgmental, self-righteous and critical can be extremely destructive — and is as dangerous as any other sin. How do we avoid that? By putting our eyes on our Lord, instead of on other men.

This doesn't mean that we are to enter lives of solitude — avoiding men and meditating only on Jesus. We cannot disobey the Bible's strong urgings to seek the fellowship of believers. Nor does it mean that we are not to trust our evangelists, teachers, pastors or shepherds. It just means that Jesus alone is worthy. Worthy, worthy is the Lamb that was slain. Men fail. Jesus will not. Men fail in the battle for holiness and fall victim to the corrupters.

But Jesus did not. And there's the answer.

Let's keep our eyes on Him. God never intended it to be any other way.

Praise His name! As we learn to listen to God's voice, some of us must be prepared for what may seem to be silence. But it may not be silence at all! We just have to relearn to *recognize the voice of our shepherd!*

Others of us may have to learn for the first time what is the voice of the Lord. What a joy when we genuinely begin to know the gentle, calming, inner voice of the Lord.

And many of us need to learn to discern it from that inner voice of ego — or demonic deception — which tells us that we have a great spiritual truth — *when we have nothing at all.*

How to spot a cult

You might be surprised that I would attack Christian humanism and ignore blatant secular humanism in the Church — such as that of church leaders who doubt the virgin birth and resurrection of Jesus.

And what about the rampant heresy that God no longer speaks to Christians today? Beware of such teachers! Recently, a dear lady proclaimed that the dictionary definition of a cult was *any group that claimed to receive revelation for today*.

The Bible certainly makes no such distinction! Instead, we are urged to listen to prophets and use our God-given discernment and our knowledge of the Word to determine if their revelations are divine.

Let me give you a better definition of a cult:

Any supposedly Christian group whose leaders claim to have all the answers for their followers, whose members are urged to avoid contact with Christians outside their group and whose teaching holds that wise founders of the faith years ago established all the necessary doctrines and that we do not need to search out God's truth for ourselves.

If you are in such a group, beware! Listen to what the Apostle Paul warned in Romans 16:17, 18:

> *"...Stay away from those who cause divisions and are upsetting people's faith ... Such teachers are not working for our Lord Jesus, but only want gain for themselves. They are good speakers, and simple-minded people are often fooled by them."*

And, of course, there are such new heresies as reconstructionism. This unbiblical theology teaches the Church will triumph and claim the "crown rights" of Jesus Christ before the Second Coming.

In the reconstructed society, government will be a democratic republic. The Bible will be the constitution.

That sounds nice until you begin scratching under the surface. There you find such oddities as "biblical slavery" in which debtors labor away their indebtedness. And then you find an intense legalism in which the old Jewish law becomes the law of the land! This stuff is being taught in Church!

In Isaiah 1:23, 26, then 3:14, 15, the sin of Judah is blamed foremost on the shepherds, pastors and leaders. Isaiah 9:17 includes the lay people who went astray by their own sins. The consequences of sin are inevitable, but the full responsibility lies with the shepherds — which Isaiah says were as guard dogs which did not bark.

An irony is how some Christian leaders will turn their back on faith — declaring that God is dead — then get caught up in the occult, which requires just as much faith and certainly an added measure of gullibility.

The late Bishop James Pike at one time seemed to be a serious Christian thinker. Then he began doubting different tenets of the Christian faith. At one point he said that he could sing the Apostle's Creed but that he could not conscientiously say it — because he could no longer accept what it said.

Bishop Pike then turned his attention to summoning demonic spirits.

A lovely pastime for a clergyman, you might say. He apparently got interested in spiritism soon after he became an Episcopal priest. He heard strange noises in his parsonage in Poughkeepsie, New York.

In England, he heard more strange noises and found books and other objects inexplicably moved about behind locked doors. Bishop Pike gave spiritualism and occultism a tremendous boost when he took part in a television seance with the famous medium, Arthur Ford. Through this and other dealings with mediums, Pike exposed millions of people to the false claims of this so-called religion — which has often been mixed up in all kinds of fakery and deceit.

When Pike disappeared in the Sinai wilderness between Israel and Egypt, his wife contacted various mediums — some of whom said he was alive and well. They shrank back into the shadows when it was discovered that he was dead.

Apparently, he had responded to "voices" that offered communication with his son, who had committed suicide. Following their instructions, he struck out into the desolate wilds, where he became disoriented and finally died of exposure and thirst.

But that's how the "friendly" spirits treat their human students. Their way is death, disappointment and destruction. They promise only enough to lure the curious to their doom. Beware! And be so, so cautious of churches which stress self-esteem and your "right to feel good about yourself." This disposition to self-assertion is the big lie that Satan has continued to use to lure man away from true fellowship with God and into a false desire of being one's own god.

Today we see this greatest lie taught right in church! And there are so many other lies that pass themselves off as forms of Christianity:

- *That each of us is the greatest being and the highest authority of what is truth. And that as the highest authority, you and I each make our own rules, for only we know what is right for us — and when it's right;*

- *That you and I can be anything we want to be if we will only believe in ourselves enough;*

- *That there are many, many paths to truth and that we must not limit ourselves to outdated — particularly fundamentalist or fanatical — ideas when it comes to religion. And certainly, we must never degrade someone else's beliefs by asserting that our own are true while theirs are false! Instead, (or so this lie goes) we should study all ways to truth as we find what is right for us, whether it is New Age neo-witchcraft or positive-thinking mind-control or Scientology or eastern mysticism or native American spiritism;*

Particularly effective has been Satan's subversion of Biblical truth:

- *The lie that missionaries destroy important primitive cultures. That natives are best left alone in the rain forests and wildernesses.*

- *The lie that "fundamentalism" is to be feared. Strict adherence to Moslem conservatism resulted in the chaos of Iran under the Ayatollah Khomeini. Thus, they say, any form of Christian "fundamentalism" is to be just as feared in America—ignoring that Islam is fundamentally centered in hatred, war, self-gratification and revenge while Christianity's fundamentals are love, peace, self-denial and forgiveness.*

- *That America was never a Christian nation.*

You and I have heard such compromises spoken as truth—while inside each of us has wanted to cry out in protest!

- *No! America was founded by Puritan pilgrims, Catholic adventurers, Baptist exiles, Quaker refugees and Anglican entrepreneurs — and many other Christians who set out to craft a society under God with freedom of religion, never freedom FROM religion. Ranging from the intensely devout Christopher Columbus to such stalwarts of the faith as Roger Williams and William Penn, American soil was consecrated and dedicated to Almighty God's will and purposes. Our country's founders were devout — despite what you have heard from those attempting to rewrite history. Washington, D.C.'s great monuments are covered with reminders of our Christian heritage. For example, the top of the Washington Monument proclaims in Latin: "Praise God!" Furthermore, America has been a beacon of hope, sending out more missionaries and real aid to the downtrodden than any nation in history! We are a Christian nation and we have a right to demand that our leaders return us to the proper course!*

- *No, we cannot make up our own rules. God alone is God and we are not. We must obey Him and follow His way whether we find it in His Word, the Bible — or obey His still, small voice called conscience ... which in this day is too often confused with "righteous rationalization" as we convince ourselves that wrong is right — and as we lie to ourselves that the Holy Spirit led us to do evil.*

- *No, we are not the highest beings. We will never be gods. We are humble creations put here to commune with, worship, glorify and obey our Lord God, the only Master of the Universe who sent His son, Jesus Christ, to show us the way to eternal life and peace with our fellow man!*

- *Yes, since we are created in God's glorious image, each of us has wonderful gifts and talents and callings ... but we can only succeed with God's daily one-to-one help, by learning His ways and by yielding to His comforting Spirit as daily we seek His marvelous plan for each of us.*

- *Success cannot be measured in power, acclaim or wealth. Our Lord calls us to deny all that.*

- *Each of us is called to use our God-given gifts to win the lost. No excuses will hide the shame of the disobedient when the sky is rolled back on the Day of Judgment and the great, betraying lies of Lucifer are instantly bared before all mankind.*

A friend brought me an advertisement from a well-known book club. "Put the Power of the Occult at Your Command!" the advertisement says. There follows a magical mixture of books, tarot cards, numerology games, astrology charts — everything imaginable to involve people in the dark side. Everywhere things of this kind are coming out into the open. In the streets of Rome and Los Angeles witches march, demanding the right to practice their rites openly. In England and Europe graves are opened, tombstones are broken, churches are desecrated, debasing acts are performed.

In America, Satan is worshiped! More and more psychics are winning popular approval. In California a man with allegedly psychic powers recently came to a prominent university to try to prove that his powers exist. It was claimed that he can read minds, bend keys and snap spoons without touching them, and even repair watches by unknown powers. He says that he does not think such power comes from his mind: "I believe it is generated through me by an intelligent power in the universe. I believe in God, but I do not believe this is coming from God."

If these strange abilities come from some intelligent power in the universe which is not God ... what is that power?

I think you know.

Brothers and sisters, before we do anything in the name of Almighty God, we must seek Him humbly and fervently. We must examine the problem in light of the Word.

Not in our *human* understanding. Nor in our *human* strength.

But in **His** wisdom.

As you consider this, is your *human* intellect a curse? *Certainly not.* Otherwise, there would not be so many biblical admonitions to study the Scriptures and to meditate on the Lord. But when we take action on our intellect alone — or emotions alone — without divine guidance, we undertake spiritual warfare without a Commander.

We dive into battle without hearing His command, without being guaranteed assistance and without receiving any divine strategy. We charge the devil's windmills in our own strength, waging war where we have no commission to go.

As a result, our wounded lie all around us today. We point accusing fingers at them and each other.

"Obviously something must be wrong," we shout. But it must be the other guy's tactics — not ours.

After all, **our** hearts are pure. In reality, we have allowed our hearts to be corrupted with presumption, self-righteousness and religiosity. Once our hearts are stolen away from Jesus Christ, lusts of the flesh — such as egos-run-amuck — take His rightful place. We put our eyes on money and fame and glory and men — even good Christian leaders. We adopt a glittery "celebrity Christianity" or a dead cult of the Christian intellect.

We downplay repentance *rather than deal with the sinful lusts of our own human hearts* — or else take the wildly opposite course, attempting to be Christian Pharisees adhering sternly to the law. And all too often, we turn from one teacher to the next, hoping for a message that won't require us to examine our hearts, our motives and our actions, but which will give us self-gratification, excitement, confirmation, wealth or status among our Christian peers.

We ignore Christian discipline and commitment. We take no positions of service — such as working as Sunday school teachers, intercessors, ushers, street evangelists or visitors to shut-ins. Instead, we become "feed-me, feed-me Christians" believing that we can fulfill our needs by standing in prayer lines and responding again and again to altar calls. OR — we swing to the other extreme, becoming entirely works- and service-oriented, latching onto human rules, requirements, creeds, denominations and theologies. We try to work our way into God's grace by our good works. We put our eyes on man's guidelines as we search for new and better answers. We try out human solutions to such simple dilemmas as Sunday school curriculum or as grandiose as worldwide hunger.

The corruption is just as terrible on one side of the theological fence as it is on the other. Charismatics and Pentecostals are inflicted with prophets purporting to declare messages from the Lord — which too frequently come only from the prophet.

In fundamentalist and evangelical churches, the prophetic mantle is taken up by theologians who proclaim exciting human inventions justified by Biblical truths taken out of context.

In Catholic circles, the humanism inserts itself as tradition. Like Tevye the milkman in "The Fiddler on the Roof," devout, sincere Christians find themselves answering challenges with shouts of "Tradition!" Why do we do this or that? Well ... because we have always done this or that! *Tradition!*

Yet, my friend, if the tradition has human origins and if it conflicts with what the Bible teaches — then it is Christian humanism.

No, this problem is not new. Ever since the Garden of Eden, man has always warmed to the idea that he knows more than God — *or at least that he has sufficient God-given wisdom to strike out on his own without divine involvement.*

I'm talking about Christians who seem to think that they can coast along on a past religious experience and be ensured of God's support on whatever human plan they undertake. *But be warned:* **You and I get into trouble when we fail to take everything we do before the Lord.**

I'm also talking about Christian leaders who take the evangelism battle into their own human hands. We Christian soldiers have a Commander. We must wait patiently for permission to attack! And even then we must pray fervently for His blessing on each detail of our battle plan. You and I get into enormous difficulties when we start making up orders to be executed in our own wisdom and strength.

Rationalization of evil creeps in quickly. We end up telling ourselves that our cause is *just* and, so, almost any course of warfare is permissible, given our noble objectives.

How many times have you seen legitimate ministries take this to the extreme — for example, fighting their financial woes with human-created deceptions and manipulating trusting supporters with false announcements of this crisis or that urgent need?

Be warned again: You and I get into terrible trouble when we fail to take everything we do before the Lord. I'm also talking about Christian leaders who say that we can cure our Church's many afflictions by retreating to man-made doctrines and traditions — which seemingly worked before. This popular diagnosis says we must return to correct theological fundamentals of the faith and basic moral ethics.

Well, of course. But the problem here is: What man shall we choose to tell us which fundamentals are of God and which are human heresies?

Paul warned the church in Corinth against hurrying after one teacher or another — dividing the brotherhood into camps bickering over different human answers.

> "Now I beseech you, brethren ... that there be no divisions among you. ...for it hath been declared unto me of you that there are contentions among you.
> "Now this I say, that every one of you saith, I am of Paul; and I of Apollos; and I of Cephas; and I of Christ.
> "Is Christ divided? Was Paul crucified for you?

> *"Or were ye baptized in the name of Paul?*
> *"I thank God that I baptized none of you … lest any should say that I had baptized in mine own name" (I Cor. 1:10-15 King James Version).*

Throughout the centuries our human tendency to follow after men instead of Jesus Christ has served to divide our great house of the Lord — to the delight of hell's minions. From the very first, Christian teachers have been tempted to explain the Scriptures in their own human intellect. The Epistles are all full of warnings to the early Church not to follow after this false interpretation of certain teachers or that human teaching of various Christian leaders.

In recent Christian history, we've all seen the problem magnify itself:

• *One man decides that in order to be a true believer, we must dress differently and live a simple life. So, off he goes with his band of followers, self-righteously pointing accusing fingers back at those who will not listen.*

• *Another man announces that in order to be true Christians, we must ban all instrumental music from our worship. So, off he goes, separating himself from like believers — denouncing all who remain as deceived of Satan.*

• *And still another man begins teaching that in order to follow the Lord, we must organize the Church into an incredible corporate structure with authoritarian shepherds helping the flock decide if it is the right time for them to marry or buy a new car or discipline their children.*

Very respected men are declaring before our divided brotherhood that the Church must solve its current problems by:

• *Exorcising emotionalism from worship;*

• *Divorcing ourselves from the "hyper-faith, greed gospel" of those who emphasize those scriptural passages that indicate God would have us prosper materially;*

• *Associating only with Christians who properly teach this or that interpretation of the Book of Revelation;*

- *Purging anything from our worship or prayer life that has the slightest similarity to any false counterparts in pagan religions — regardless whether our legitimate practices are rooted in the Word of God and were practiced by the Apostles and early church; and*

- *Undoing the damage of two decades of emphasis on faith and the Holy Spirit — particularly the idea that God still speaks to us, or will heal illness, or raise the dead, or restore the maimed.*

I say that this preposterous list is not of the Lord — and is the result of nothing but Christian humanism, which was one of the earliest corruptions in the Church:

"... no prophecy recorded in Scripture was ever thought up by the prophet himself. It was the Holy Spirit within these godly men who gave them true messages from God" (II Peter 1:20-21).

Christian humanism results when men decide what God wants His people to do. I'm sure that sounds like a terrible sin — very close to false prophecy — which was punished in the Old Testament by stoning the false prophet behind the city gates! However, its modern version is the greatest temptation of the Christian teacher. *Why?* Because those of us to whom believers turn for answers *want* to be able to give those answers.

One insidious form of Christian humanism says God does not speak anymore and we lonely humans must find our own answers in our intellectual interpretation of the Scriptures. It says we are to use the Bible as a guidebook to be dissected just as Jewish scholars nit-picked the Old Testament into volumes and volumes of intricate religious rules, regulations and definitions.

Why is this practice wrong?

Because we cannot depend on the Bible *alone.* Like it or not, we are all human beings with human failings. If we try to read the Bible in our human wisdom *alone,* we will come up with all sorts of inner conflicts. Only empowered by the Holy Spirit and in humility before our great Lord God can we to seek His answers in the Word.

Carefully read a little poem (even if you hate poetry):

> For the preaching of the cross
> is to them that perish
> **foolishness;**
> But unto us which are saved it is **the power of God.**
> For it is written, I will destroy the **wisdom of the wise,**
> and will bring to nothing the **understanding of the
>   prudent.**
>
> Where is the wise?
> Hath not God made foolish the wisdom of this world?
> For ... the world **by wisdom** knew not God.
> It pleased God
> by the **foolishness of preaching**
> to save them that believe.
> ... Because the foolishness of God is wiser than men;
> and the weakness of God is stronger than men.
> For ye see ... brethren, how that not many
>   wise men after the flesh,
> not many **mighty,** not many **noble,** are called.
> But God hath chosen the foolish things of the world
>   to confound the wise ...
> That no flesh should glory in his presence...
>
> He that glorieth, let him glory in the Lord.
> And I, brethren, when I came to you,
> came not with excellency of speech or of wisdom, declar-
>   ing unto you the testimony of God.
> For I determined not to know any thing among you,
> save Jesus Christ, and him crucified.
>
> And I was with you in weakness, and in fear, and in
>   much trembling. And my speech and my preaching
>   was not with enticing words of man's wisdom,
> but in demonstration of the Spirit and of power:
> That your faith should not stand in the wisdom of men,
>   but in the power of God.

Who is the poet of that bit of wisdom? The Apostle Paul, in
passages excerpted from I Corinthians 1:18-31 of the beautiful King James Version.

What is Paul's point here?

He was attempting to explain to the church in Corinth just why all their bickering and following after different men's human doctrines was an exercise in foolishness.

Yes, brothers and sisters, we have a problem. It is our human nature. It has brought down some of God's greatest servants in humiliation and shame.

Run amock, it plays into Satan's hand. Our natural lust for money, fame, applause, power and acclaim is not God's plan for us. Yes, it is time we woke up and learned from history. We have violated God's laws. We need to reexamine the faith of our forefathers. We need to humble ourselves in brokenness, willing to sacrifice all —

And not long to be Christian superstars.

Superstars, heroes and idols

The Christian superstar with whom I was to appear was immensely pleasant and smooth. His conversation was incredibly "spiritual."

He said all the correctly religious things at the right time. He had churchly lingo down pat.

But as he and I talked, I began to notice little giveaways — the way he carried himself, they way he held eye contact, the way he responded to my one-on-one attempts to minister to him ... and how my own spirit cried out within me that something was very wrong about this young "spiritual giant."

On stage, his message was loud and clear, wrapped in glittering pseudo-Christianity. But backstage, it was clearer still — screaming the true nature of his heart. He could not hide his secret behind fancy words or religious phrases.

He was incredibly arrogant toward everyone. Puffed up. Vicious. Frantically, he pushed his odd theological viewpoints on me — whom he apparently respected as a hero or role model. He desperately fought for my attention.

I began to hurt for him. It was tragic to see a brother trying to fake the business of God, desperately attempting to impress me and receive my smile — my acceptance, my assurance that his ministry was legitimate.

I realized he was in agony. Since I enjoy running each morning, I invited him to join me at dawn. Out on the trail, he resumed his antics and pushy ways. I felt I had no choice but to confront him in brotherly love. With great caution and deep respect, I expressed to him my perception of his fear that his false spirituality would be detected. I shared with him my concerns about his heart. I showed him how I had discerned his true attitudes. I expressed to him that he must come clear with the Lord — that such false spirituality would eventually destroy his public ministry and, more importantly, lose him his soul.

He sneered at me in sudden hatred. He denied all and accused me of professional jealousy. He scoffed at my Christian discernment and accused me and all other evangelists of being fakes, con artists and religious showmen.

As he turned away from me and jogged back to his hotel, I was disappointed, but not terribly surprised. So many people in ministry are in such terrible shape these days. You find them full of "love" on the outside — particularly when the TV cameras are focused in.

But inside, they are actors — hustlers playing the angles of their own imaginary religious game show — saying all the right things at the right times. So many are so full of "righteous anger" toward other Christian leaders. Loudly and viciously they pass public judgment on others. They point out the others' terrible flaws, theological errors and violations of religious "rules."

I'd like to note that the life of a Christian superstar is not an easy one. For years I stayed on the road, my life seemingly belonging to everyone but me. I became exhausted — emotionally, spiritually and physically. Burned out.

And I became frustrated as people called me a great hero.

Just what did I ever to do be considered a hero? I'm a rejected kid who God chose to put into the ministry. By the grace of our Lord, I was allowed to win my witchcraft-practicing mother and father and brothers and sisters into God's kingdom — and we are going to have one great family reunion in heaven. *But that doesn't make me a hero.* Read the Book of Hebrews if you want to learn about heroes. Read the Book of Acts. Those people put their lives on the line for their faith. What is a hero?

Noah was a hero. He withstood years of ridicule as he dedicatedly stuck to a seemingly absurd project — because God told him to build an ark and try to fill it with people who would be saved from the terrible judgment coming. The people laughed and refused to repent. But because of his faith,

Noah was counted by God to be a great man. Abraham was a hero. God told him to leave his comfortable home and be the founder of a holy nation in unknown regions.

Another hero would be Joseph. He was betrayed by his brothers and sold into slavery. Tempted by his boss's wife, he remained pure and spent years in prison — forgotten by his accusers — for refusing to commit adultery. When given incredible opportunities to take terrible vengeance on his brothers, he forgave them. That's a hero.

Moses was a hero.

John the Baptist was a hero.

Stephen was a hero.

But let me tell you who is not a hero. All around us today, our heroes are sad counterfeits. Movie stars. Soap opera actors. Musicians. Performers.

John Wayne was not a hero, friends. He was a great actor. But he didn't lay down his life for anybody. What about Oliver North? He followed his convictions, then refused to tell self-serving politicians what he had done. But I don't think that puts him in the same category as Moses, John or Stephen.

Me, I'm just a preacher. *A preacher who is disturbed when I hear another term bantered about, too:*

Idol.

I've actually heard a well-known Christian performer called a "Christian rock music teen idol. "

Whoa! Wait a minute.

Let's be very careful about setting anyone up — particularly a Christian — as an idol.

None of us, regardless of our message, talent or personal charisma deserve to become idols.

Idols are worshiped without scrutiny.

Perhaps, my friends, that's one of our brotherhood's problems. We've set up idols — Christian idols — and required nothing of them. We lavish them with our gifts. We adore them with our praises.

And we ask no questions. But here is another great sin that we commit: So many pastors and evangelists desperately need your friendship. They need to be invited into your home and given a chance to be just a fellow Christian. Why do I mention this? Because so many preachers and their spouses are incredibly lonely. People put them on a pedestal and look to them for inspiration, guidance and wisdom.

Yet, these pastors and evangelists need close friends.

Remember Bebe Rebozo? His single claim to history is that he was Richard Nixon's buddy. When quizzed by the news media, he generally responded with the most nonchalant of reports of the President's personal life. The two of them sat around and watched football. Or went sailing. Or golfing.

Nixon, one of American history's truly tragic figures, depended on Rebozo not for foreign relations insights or guidance on the economy or how to end the war in Vietnam. Instead, Rebozo was just a good ol' boy, around whom Richard Nixon was just one of the guys.

Your pastor — or his wife or his kids — may need you to be a Bebe Rebozo. Just a friend. If you don't think that's your calling, try this:

Pray for your pastor daily. Pray specifically. *Listen* to his conversations with you. Is he concerned about his daughter's grades? Then pray for her to excel and make her daddy proud. Does he mention the transmission on his car? His noisy air conditioner? His unhappy mother, widowed 1,000 miles away? Lift up those needs. Ask the Lord to show you what — if anything — you should do about them.

And what about those superstars on Christian TV?

Pray for them, too. Ask the Lord to show you what to pray for.

Lift them up. They're just people. They make mistakes. Very few of them actually are money-grubbing con-artists.

The vast majority desperately seek to serve the Lord effectively.

Many are caught up in enormous financial troubles.

You may not know the inner terror that comes over even the most faithful man of God when his bookkeeper drops the bombshell that offerings are off 90 percent and this month, the ministry is in debt $500,000 to TV stations.

You can be a giant of faith, yet find yourself stirred by the horrible possibilities.

It's truly a terrible thing to believe with all your heart and soul that the Lord has told you to step out in faith and go $250,000 in debt — only to discover that you did the wrong

thing and that it was your flesh speaking, not the Father.
You find yourself filled with self-doubt. How could you have
misunderstood the Lord's voice?

Do you, indeed, know what He sounds like?

Have you made an incredible error in believing that you
have a legitimate ministry? What makes you think that you
have anything to say that anybody needs to hear?

Oh, yes, it can be lonely. Particularly if you have gone into
the ministry for all the wrong reasons, anyway.

It was painful and frustrating for me to see my running
partner's great emptiness.

Why do such young idols enter the ministry?

Do they think this is some game?

Don't they know that God — whose great and terrible
wrath is nothing to be trifled with — will hold them accounta-
ble? Christianity is no game. Evangelizing the lost requires
selflessness — not flaming egos!

Ah, Nicky, you may be saying, don't judge him so harshly.

Ah, yes.

That's really not my job, is it?

I just need to love the kid — despite my great irritation at
his combative religiosity.

Preaching Jesus is no game.

Christianity is not meant to be competitive.

Competitive Christianity. You've seen it. And it is so destructive! It breeds the sorts of evil that I remember in my
native Puerto Rico when television finally arrived. It came in
the mid-1950s just as the island's economy was improving
somewhat.

With a new degree of prosperity our little island in the Caribbean got a big dose of materialism and greed. Although
Puerto Ricans are U.S. citizens, they have a Latin heritage
that runs deep — including that hispanic phenomenon called
"machismo."

What it amounts to is a deep, deep need for men to constantly assert and prove their manhood — particularly to
themselves!

This time machismo brought a desperate competition to
"keep up with the Joneses." A man was not truly a man if he

could not afford to buy his family a car — and certainly a
much nicer car than anyone else on his street. His kids had to
dress much nicer, too. And if somebody else's kids started taking piano lessons, look out! Soon the kids next door would be
taking **organ** lessons! The only problem with this was that
Puerto Rico is a relatively low-income area. And this time, not
everybody could afford to keep up.

One neighborhood in particular was already in severe financial trouble because of all the competition. Then one of the
homeowners got a wonderful new status symbol — a
television!

Everyone on the block was so impressed. The kids chat-
tered in excitement. The women were so envious. The men
were so humiliated. They had to get TVs, too. Somehow. One
husband just flatly told his wife that enough was enough.
They could not afford another big expense. A TV was out of
the question. But even as he said it, he peered out the window
at the gleaming antenna. He ground his teeth covetously. His
shame was more than he could bear.

"Oh, honey," **whined the woman,** "if you really loved me,
you would buy me a TV. You're every bit the man that he is
— aren't you? I believe you can find a way. I believe you can
do it. Can't you? Please? For me?"

"No," muttered the man, his face red.

But his wife didn't give up. The subject came up over
supper.

"No," snapped the man. "We cannot afford it. There is no
way within our budget. They only way we can do it is just to
wait maybe a year."

"A year?" **wailed the wife.** "I cannot bear it. Everyone will
have a TV before we do! A year! You tell me that the neighbors — with that big, fat, lazy husand of hers — can afford a
TV when we can't? Oh, honey! Remember what you said
about all the other nice things that we have. You said we
couldn't afford them, either! But we managed to find a way."

"Look, woman!" yelled the man, "it's because of all these
other things that we can't afford even one more thing. Nothing more. Nothing. And I don't want to hear another word
about it."

But it came up again after supper. This time, the woman wept and wailed and threatened to invite her mother to come stay for a month. Mama would figure out away if the husband could not!

And as the poor man climbed into bed, you can be sure that it came up again. So, the unfortunate husband had no choice. His honor, his manhood, his peace of mind — and certainly his peace and quiet — were at stake. So the next day, he brought home a wonderful package in a great, big box.

As the neighbors gawked in amazement, he crawled up on the roof and installed an enormous, beautiful television antenna — much bigger and certainly much shinier than the one next door. Proudly his wife chatted with all the other women, bragging about how prosperous her husband had made their family since he made so much money at his truly important job. And neither husband nor wife gave a single hint of their dark, terrible secret.

The antenna was connected to nothing. He had brought home no TV — just the antenna — an expensive ornament bought to impress and amaze. *Some Christians are just like that.*

They put on big shows. They put on enormous pretense to impress the world that they have something ... which they do not have at all. They want to be superstars.

But God is not impressed with superstars. Just look at Samson.

The first superstar

Samson was a superstar even before be became a full-grown man. God ordained him to be the strongest person who ever lived. Samson had strength like no man before him. He had charm. He was a natural leader. He was born to lead Israel.

But instead of being one of the Bible's greatest heroes, he is one of history's most bitter disappointments. Why?

He misused his special gifts and anointing. He wasted his talents. He got out of line and corrupted his calling. He let his lusts run unchecked. He seemingly decided that as God's chosen deliverer of Israel he could do no wrong.

He was mistaken.

The Lord lifted the anointing.

Samson was permitted to fall.

In his enormous disgrace, Samson not only let himself down, but he took Israel down with him. When Samson finally stood on display in the Philistine temple — blinded, weakened, defeated and mocked by his enemies, he finally repented. He called on God, the only true source of his power, and in a final moment of glory defeated Israel's oppressors.

Samson's story is being repeated over and over around us today. They are born leaders, good-looking, able to impact a nation with their actions. They have been touched by God in a special way for a designated, specific purpose. They have been equipped by God with great gifts and special graces for the purpose of revealing to this world the Living God.

But many of them have not been responsible with God's

anointing in their lives. Many of them have lost God's blessing. Others can't remember even having it. They deny the ex-
istence of the supernatural and rely on their natural abilities
to spread the Gospel.

I believe this is one of the reasons why so many Christians
are in their own "Philistine dungeon." They are crushed, lonely and confused in their deception, because they got out of line
with God. Therefore, many of them begin to rely on their own
charisma, the glamor of their personal magnetism and well-
practiced eloquence.

Yet, they are only empty exorcisers. They have no meaning,
no real message and no power to change a dying world full of
lost people.

If you look closely into these people's private families and
home lives, you will find them to be depressing or disastrous.
They live lives full of problems and paranoia. They are neuro-
tic. They have serious child-parent problems. They are consumed with financial problems.

And they lie.

Why do Christian hustlers degrade us all with false
claims? Why do they try to project bogus images of Christlike-
ness — only to be exposed to the shame of us all? Why do
they constantly strive to impress others, themselves and —
apparently — God?

One of the first clues of such people is a sneering attitude
about other ministries. I've seen this in those who reach out
to prison inmates and in those who minister on the streets —
two vitally effective ministries that Satan is determined to
discredit and destroy.

It seems as if there is some bizarre competition to detail
a criminal past or delinquent childhood far worse than anyone
else's — as well as a Christian conversion experience incredibly more dramatic than anyone else's. Along with their own
wild claims, they confide the supposed false nature of their
counterparts' testimonies. In particular, they slander the larg-
er, more effective ministries.

I've seen this terrible competition in operations ranging
from anti-drug outreaches to praise-and-worship music
publishers.

Why? Why must Christians feel the need to destroy one another? Because struggling as they are in their own power and without the comforting presence of God's Holy Spirit active in their lives, they genuinely feel threatened by the other similar ministries.

Thus, they must degrade and discredit the competition in order to look good. Because the Lord is not in their lives, they are blind to the fact that they only discredit themselves.

After watching such professional "religionists," I've noticed another pattern.

Little by little, they cease even pretending to live the Christian lifestyle when their success as traveling evangelists allows them to slip into increasing comfort and convenience. And when someone is sent by the Lord to exhort them to righteousness, they become indignant and vengeful. They go on the attack. It is wisest to leave them alone.

But then, you must leave these sheepskin-clad wolves alone in the midst of the flock.

So, what can you and I do?

Join the denouncers? **No.**

Pray for them. *Fervently.*

Pray for God's blessing and touch and truth.

Don't condemn them before the throne of God,

Ask that God touch their hearts in a *special* way.

When you encounter such pride in a Christian leader, ask the Lord to convict him or her of the fact that they are hurting God's people. Pray that they will see that as public Christian figures, they are entrusted with the moral and ethical revival of this nation.

If they persist in being such terrible examples, many will seek a way other than Jesus. Others will follow them — believing that extravagance and lust are the Christian way.

Off course, they are not. To claim so is a lie.

But these bogus spiritual giants don't mind a little falsehood. They copy Christians' words and gestures and fabricate a false way devoid of the blood of Jesus Christ. You and I can both think of a good-looking TV host who seemingly could do no wrong. Everything he touched prospered. Where he led, people followed. Perhaps you are thinking of a local Christian TV celebrity. Or maybe you're thinking of a national one whose fall was more surrounded in notoriety. But both men found their own Delilah. And like Samson, they were humiliated and shorn of their power. Bright, charming leaders, they were equipped by our Lord with great gifts and special talents for purposes of revealing to this world the Living God.

But they were seduced by their own lusts and pride. They began to believe they were the great men of God that the adoring audiences said they are. They were deceived, believing that the Lord's power in their lives is their own strength.

For this reason so many humiliated Christians live out their lives chained in Philistine temples — mocked by the world, powerless to do anything about their shame. They are crushed, lonely and confused in their humiliation.

Why?

Because they got out of line with God. They tried to rely on their own personal charisma — not the power of the Holy Spirit. They wove pretty deceptions of their own with high-tech wonders and eloquent words written by strangers.

They are too proud to see that they are only empty vessels without the power to affect a dying world. They got out of line with God. They stepped out of His plan. They violated His laws.

And outside of His blessing and protection, they struggle along with their empty ministries. Their lives are full of secret disgrace and a growing fear that followers will learn of their emptiness.

They are terrified of being exposed — shunning close contact with believers and fleeing even the Christian press. They only make public appearances when they control the cameras and the microphones. Their families are in disarray. Their marital relationships are in ruins.

Their finances are in constant crisis.

Yet, God's people continue to follow them.

Why?

Remember what Jesus called the Church? Remember what he told Peter to do — repeatedly: "Feed my sheep."

Barnyard sheep do not have any natural leadership ability — nor even a sense of direction.

They need a shepherd.

We need God-sent shepherds.

What happens when you put your eyes on men?

Kevin was about 20 years old and quite impressionable. He was very taken with one of today's more prominent TV preachers — and believed that he should spend his life assisting in this man's ministry. Kevin's friends heard him talk of little else. He mimicked the man's style of preaching. He copied his hard-hitting approach on doctrinal issues and even began combing his hair like the evangelist did.

Those who knew and loved Kevin were concerned. It did not seem wise to sort out the strengths and weaknesses of his hero — and show Kevin that the evangelist was just a man. Those who heard Kevin talk sometimes began to wonder "What about Jesus in his life?" He didn't talk much about Jesus. He didn't seem to be nearly as excited about the Christ.

Of course, Kevin knew Jesus. It was just that this certain Christian leader was a real, tangible, flesh-and-blood role model for Kevin. Kevin was young enough that this didn't seem terribly unhealthy. He would learn. *He would see.*

And the Lord would pick up the pieces — at least that's what everyone assumed. But one day, the evangelist fell from grace.

The press was filled with stories of how he had swindled little old ladies out of millions of dollars. A TV news show showed his wife bragging about his wealth on hidden camera — and had the evangelist denying that he owned a cent in the world ... then admitting that he did have a "former" role in a string of retirement homes.

Kevin was devastated. At first, he was the evangelist's greatest defender. Then, when federal indictments said he had

stolen millions of dollars from elderly Christians — and when
the evangelist mounted stall tactics to keep from repaying any
of the money — Kevin fell silent.

He quit preaching. He took a job as a clerk in a large national
discount store. Within months, he was put into management
training. He soon was the head of his own store, then a district
supervisor — particularly effective in working with young management trainees who had little direction in their lives. The
store became Kevin's life. *He helped them make it theirs.*

Today Kevin doesn't have much time for church. He will
smile and roll his eyes when reminded of the days when he had
such high ambitions to be a great evangelist.

"We were all young and foolish once," he says wryly.

What a terrible thing. What a loss to the Kingdom!
What a horrible judgment must await the evangelist who betrayed Kevin's trust and dreams in return for a few dollars.

I've seen the tenderness of young evangelists trying to follow
me, too. What a responsibility! As best I can, I turn their attention to Jesus. I am so imperfect. I cannot have a fine young
man expecting me to be Jesus Christ.

If your faith is centered around one preacher or one TV evangelist, I urge you to get down on your knees and thank the Lord
for the One that He sent to be crucified.

Jesus Christ. Then, keep your eyes on Him.

Jesus was a man like you and me. But He never disappoints
… like you and I do.

That may seem hard-hearted. But the best thing I can do is
to be a faithful friend and advisor as I constantly turn my
would-be disciples' eyes on Jesus. They don't need to tour the
Soviet Union with me. They need to get alone in the wilderness
with their Lord.

I know I'm not the only evangelist to face this challenge. It is
so tempting! Your ego swells with self-importance and self-
confirmation: yes, indeed, I am a mighty, holy man of God. This
fine young man I have raised up is proof.

No! It is not! So many of these young ministers are vulnerable to those who would use them for their own gain. They open
themselves freely to the Gospel and to God's purposes for their
lives — just as we all should.

But they don't challenge the wrong they surely see. Expect-

ing and believing the best of we, their role models, they invest in
us great trust. They believe whatever we say. They choose to
view only the facade that many evangelists exhibit for the world
to see.

They do not question the condition of our hearts. But
they must! I am not telling anyone to set themselves up as judge
and jury, but Christians are given discernment for a reason!

We are given our ability to study and divide the Word of truth
for a holy purpose! Listen to what the Spirit is telling you when
you sense something is wrong with a ministry! Do not close your
eyes! Do not pretend that you do not see! Certainly, you cannot
begin attacking the Lord's anointed men of God just because you
suspect something isn't quite right. But neither can you ignore
that still, small voice that is urging you to trust in Jesus, not imperfect men.

These young men want to believe that everything in the
Church is good and godly. They want to believe that there is no
lust for money or fame or recognition or applause.

They want to believe that there is no jockeying for position, no
artful manipulation of the trusting flock. They see no politics —
although the religion industry is full of it. They see no racial dis-
crimination — although it is there in its great ugliness. They
see no selfish ambition, no immorality, no love of wealth, no desire to rule over people.

Perhaps this very same idealism that makes them so vulnerable drives them to win the lost and change the world. But why
do they need a "mentor" — a hero? Isn't Jesus enough?

They want someone who will take them under a wing and
show them all truth and the intricacies of God's way. Many ea-
gerly desire to enter into a relationship similar to that of Jesus
and His disciples.

Yet, this is not healthy. I am not our Lord. Neither is any other evangelist. But it is so fulfilling to have a "Timothy" tagging
along behind, trying so hard to be your right hand man.

What happens when a young man blindly puts his life in control of an untrustworthy mentor? My heart breaks when I see
idealistic young Timothies unquestioningly adopting their men-
tors' philosophies about pride, ensuring personal financial gain
first, holding onto tradition since it's "what people want," to
play with people's emotions and to doctor the truth to make a

good testimony even better. Look at all the recent scandals we have had. Many leaders are practicing the philosophy that the end justifies the means.

Wrong. The Lord won't bless that. If such practices are prospering, then the source is other than heavenly.

It troubles me terribly when I see these young Timothies being taught self-righteous pride.

"We are clergy," is the attitude. "We are the high priests. We understand the higher things and explain them to the rabble." Wrong. Pride will just get you into enormous trouble.

I was invited to speak in a certain city. A week before the date, I sent one of my staff members to check on the arrangements. "Find out what they've been doing to advertise the crusade," I told Bill. "Also how many prayer chains have been set up for support. Check on the size of the auditorium, the lighting — you know, all those little things that are so important to our crusades."

Bill went, but when he reported back to me he looked so dejected I couldn't understand it. "What's the trouble, Bill?" I asked. "You look as though you're ready to write a new song:

"I have the gloom, gloom, gloom, gloom — down in my heart!"

"I suppose so," Bill said with a sigh. "I just can't take any more of what I've been through."

Bill explained that when he had arrived at the scene of my coming crusade, he had been treated, he felt, like dirt. There were good plans under way, but every suggestion Bill made to improve them was rejected outright. The local crusade committee took a totally negative attitude toward everything Bill said; nothing could be added to or taken away from their plans — not even the smallest detail.

Result: I had to go to the crusade site earlier than I had planned, simply to do what the committee hadn't let Bill do.

The instant I arrived, I felt as though I was being treated like visiting royalty. I made exactly the same suggestions Bill had, but this time everyone outdid themselves to do what I asked. It was too much for me. Reluctantly I took one of the committee members aside and told him how I felt about all this. "You have shamed me," I told him, "that you would treat another Christian brother as you treated Bill. You treated him completely differently from me. Yet Bill works for me. He came here as part of the crusade, part of me, and you rejected him!"

The man looked down. I think he was beginning to realize what he had done and what it would mean. For it was quite clear by now that the men of the crusade committee had been guilty of one of the worst sins of all — pride.

Pride! It is so dangerous because it is so hard to recognize. We treat some people like pieces of furniture, instead of persons, because we are so wrapped up in our own affairs that we never think of how the other person feels. We discriminate shamefully. We go out of our way to praise and please one person while we practically stomp on another.

Even our prayers can be soaked in pride. One man of prayer gave God 10 percent of his income, fasted often, and would no more have committed adultery than he would have missed church.

Yet, in his prayers this man was likely to say: "I thank you, God, that I am not greedy, dishonest, or immoral, like everybody else" (see Luke 18:9-14).

But God never heard those spiritually proud statements. We know that is one kind of prayer which God will not answer because Jesus told us so in this parable of the Pharisee and the tax collector. Look it up and you will find that Jesus tells us that God will listen more readily to the humble sinner who turns to Him than to the religious person who is filled with pride.

Pride corrupted the world in the beginning. Adam and Eve wanted to be as wise as God, and they set themselves above Him, listening to the devil's false promises instead of God's clear commands. But pride was around long before the Fall!

Satan started out as one of God's highest angels. Somewhere along the line, he developed delusions of grandeur and coveted the throne of God for himself. His unchecked pride left God no choice: He had to banish Satan —and all the rebel angels with him. One day they will be sealed up forever, but right now — as everyone who follows Jesus knows — those fallen spirits are at work night and day trying to get you and me into their wicked ranks. Since they cannot get to the Creator, they settle for the creation that most touches His heart — man!

I see the sin of pride so often — in the name-droppers, for instance. A man may come up to me and say, "When I was talking to Billy Graham and Senator Stennis recently, I thought of something Pat Boone told me about how the Lord worked in the life of Maria von Trapp."

God forgive me if I judge people like this wrongly, but I can't help being suspicious that for them I'm one more name to add to their list, so that they can tell the next person they meet, "As Nicky Cruz told me the other day .... "

And then there are the people who get in touch with me (I suspect) to make money. I am approached about so many money-making schemes, you wouldn't believe it. I turn them down because I know if I started that route, at best I would end up living for money and what it can buy, and that's not what I've given my life to God to do.

It's all a form of the old, old appeal of pride — thinking of things instead of people, thinking of yourself instead of others, putting God last instead of first.

Pride is treating somone differently because he isn't somebody. Pride is asking, "What's in it for me?' instead of, "How can I serve the Lord in this situation?" Pride is an attitude — "I can't benefit from knowing that person, or from talking to him or spending my time with him — so I won't bother with him."

But pride is not the worst thing I see our young Timothies picking up as they sit at our feet.

Insincerity is the most terrible thing they are learning. They are taught to view themselves as better than the rabble of the crowd — and to mock the congregation after services. What a conflict this creates in these idealistic young hearts! Their souls cry out for the beauty of the Lord. But their minds see it doesn't work. They begin speaking out of both sides of their mouths. They say one thing in the pulpit and at the altar, then they sneer cynically backstage.

Their hearts and spirits ache in bitter resentment, disappointment and disillusionment. They have heard the truth. But they just can't make it work.

Why? Because the human they have set their eyes on has taken his eyes off of Jesus. What happens in the end? The bright young men crash in flames.

Satan keeps whispering in their ears that none of this stuff they preach is true. "Just watch your hero," the devil reminds. "He lies. He betrays. He preaches poverty and lives like royalty. He works the crowd over like a master — wringing out their emotions and emptying their wallets. Is that what you want to be?"

And the bright young men begin to believe that although their ministy seems to produce results — hundreds of healings, thousands of conversions and millions of dollars — it's all a sham.

Sometimes the bright right-hand men crashing in flames aren't all that young.

Seeking restoration

Richard W. Dortch, 56, is the former right-hand man to PTL's Jim Bakker. Here's what he told *The Orlando Sentinel* newspaper. If you remember, Dortch was fired by Jerry Falwell for paying Jessica Hahn $265,000 in hush money during the sex scandal that brought Bakker down.

"I've asked the Church to forgive me for my errors," said Dortch.

"I've asked the public. I've asked individuals. I've asked Church leaders. I've even made my peace with Jessica. Now ... well, I don't know who else to ask. The Lord forgave the prostitute and said to her: 'Go and sin no more,' But He didn't say go where. And he didn't suggest what else she should do. That was my problem for a long while. I didn't know where to turn ... where to go, or what to do."

After finding himself defrocked by the Assemblies of God after 35 years, Dortch said he was filled with fear.

"I was, for some reason, suddenly physically afraid of people. I was scared to leave the house. Adding to that feeling was the disappointment, I'd say more of a trauma, of not getting that hug I felt I would get from my peers.

"I expected the kind of help I would have given another pastor ... had given many pastors over the years. I was known far and wide as a peacemaker, a healer of the spirit in my ministry. When help for me was not forthcoming, well, I just didn't know what to do. I was truly lost. I imagine it will take several years to sort all this out."

Didn't he ever have any inner warning about the problems at PTL? Or was it all a big surprise?

"Among the church people I knew, Bakker and his PTL group were always considered something of a loose cannon on deck. I had reservations about joining them when I was approached. It's obvious now I should have trusted those thoughts. I had no trouble with money and none with women, but when I realized I could be a part of a TV ministry that reached 30 million households, translating to maybe 50 million people, well, who wouldn't want to go along? What preacher wouldn't jump at that opportunity?

"It was a chance I couldn't let go by."

A chance he couldn't let go by.

I believe that the Lord has some incredibly productive years ahead for our brother Richard Dortch. Why? Because he has humbled himself. He has asked forgiveness.

As I write this, Dortch is living out of the spotlight. He is seeking personal healing in his own private, quiet wilderness.

Jesus used to retreat to the wilderness to pray and renew Himself.

Paul, after his conversion, disappeared into the Arabian wilderness for a long period of growing in the Lord — just as had another great man, Moses. The great deliverer, if you remember, had murdered an Egyptian in anger. Rather than face legal justice, he fled to the Sinai wilderness where he worked as a shepherd for 40 years — growing strong in the Lord in the quiet solitude of the desolate mountains.

Pray for our brother Richard Dortch.

I pray that he finds himself in a godly fellowship where he can grow in his confidence in the Lord once again.

Public disgrace is not the end of the road.

Restoration is the answer. We must restore our fallen brothers and sisters to the fold. Gradually.

Carefully. In wisdom and discernment. Who should decide when their time of renewal and restoration is complete? Certainly not the offending brother or sister. They must place themselves under the authority of good Christian elders.

However, restoring one's credibility does not happen overnight. Like it or not, we must prove ourselves to men before they will trust again with their tithes, their spiritual growth or even their attention.

Sometimes in the restoration process, we find ourselves re-

treating into the wilderness with our Lord. I've seen this hap
pen two different ways:

• God separates you for a time of seclusion and prayer. Obviously, the wilderness can be your own home. Or it can be
the Army. Or Bible college. I've seen the Lord send brothers
and sisters off away from their friends and family for a time
of preparation — often where the Christian has no choice but
to depend on God for hope, friendship and physical survival.

• Other times, you put yourself into the desert through disobedience or defiance — maybe corruption, pride, scandal ...
perhaps where you are exposed to all for having violated what
you preach. And so, you find yourself in the wilderness.
Alone. Deserted. Dependent on God alone.

Moses killed an Egyptian and banished himself to the wilderness for 40 years. He returned as the great deliverer of
Israel.

Jesus, on the other hand, knew He had to retreat into the
wilderness before beginning His ministry. He had to spend
time with the Father. There, He fasted and prayed for 40
days, was tempted, and He emerged with power and might.

Paul disappeared into the Arabian wilderness shortly after
his conversion. Little is known about his time there except
that the Lord prepared him for a completely new life   that
of missionary, writer of most of the New Testament, and ex-
emplary exhorter of the brethren.

Elijah withdrew into the wilderness to escape a murderous
king. There, he learned to depend on God for daily food.

John the Baptist vanished into the wilderness before
launching his ministry to prepare the way for the Messiah.

As I mentioned earlier, a top evangelist was approached by
my friend David Wilkerson and told to put aside his ministry
for a time and to spend time in the wilderness with God. The
evangelist responded that he wished that he could, but that
he was afraid that his multi-million dollar ministry wouldn't
be there when he returned. Wilkerson sadly left him.

Weeks later, a massive scandal took it all from the evangelist anyway. He retreated into the wilderness. Unwillingly.

But, apparently, according to God's plan for him.

So, how do you return from the wilderness? You must be
birthed by the Lord. He must make the way ready for your

return. If you come back in your own strength, you are causing your own premature birth. You'll be weak and unready.

Thus the need to place yourself under the authority of
Christian brothers who care about you.

Let them announce when the patient has recovered.

The result? Full recovery — as in the case of our brother
Fred Berry. He found himself in a dark personal wilderness,
from which many never return.

You perhaps remember Fred from the TV series *What's
Happenin'?* He was the comic character "Rerun."

I met him one evening when I was invited to speak at a
Christian drug rehabilitation program in Los Angeles. He
shared his testimony that night. He could have disappeared
in the same drug-induced fog that swallowed up John Belushi,
Len Bias, Elvis and all the others.

I was mesmerized as he rattled off all the drugs he'd been
on: reds, whites, black mollies, quaaludes, valium, cocaine,
crack, heroin, speed, ammo-nitrate and even airplane glue. He
had tried stuff I had never even heard of. He drank liquors
that you only find in exclusive shops. He had smoked everything from Maui wowie to Thai sticks.

But he got tired of being high. *He wanted more.*

He walked into a Christian detoxification center and
asked for help. Right then and there, a brother named Craig
laid hands on him — and the power of Jesus filled him. Well,
Satan wasn't too pleased about losing a client. So, if drugs
and alcohol wouldn't do the trick, perhaps money and fame
would. Just after Fred had been released from the program
and resumed his career—free of drugs and booze—he received
an incredible offer from a large beer company.

"We need you," their advertising experts told him. "We have
your personality in mind for this whole new series of commercials. We have this vision for a spectacular campaign. Just
name your price."

Believe it or not, commercials pay lots of money.

Quite a number of acting careers have been launched or re-
vived because of a successful ad. As the beer company spokesmen described their plans to Fred, he was filled with deep
sadness. They wanted him to be his jivin', be-boppin', dancin',
rappin' funniest. It would give him a chance to show off his

finest work. But, Fred knew it was all designed to sell beer to kids. He told them he would have to get back to them. *So, he thought about it.* He went to a couple of ministers in the drug program and asked their advice.

"Pray about it," they told him. He did. And he knew that there was no way that he could be part of trapping thousands of kids into booze. When the ad people called, they announced "We've chosen you. You're it. You're the one!"

"Thank you," he responded, "but NO THANK YOU."

He hung up and whispered "Thank you, God."

F*ive minutes later, they called him back.* "Fred, we really want you in this commercial," they said. "We are serious. We are so serious that we are willing to give you $60,000 to $70,000 for the first one!"

"Boy, that sounds good," said Fred. "However, the Lord is my provider. Thank you, but no thank you."

And although all his friends thought he had lost his mind, Fred said he could make no other choice. He believes that he has a special gift from God to be a role model. Other celebrities are just interested in money. But, as Fred puts it: "Hey, I didn't want to do it because children — especially children — are going to be looking at me. They are going to be following my lead — and this is not the direction I want to take them."

Just as Jesus — in His time in the wilderness — saw through Satan's traps, so did Freddie.

Jesus, who had fasted for more than a month, was tempted by Satan to turn the stones into bread. Freddie was tempted into rescuing his career and making a lot of money with a beer commercial. Jesus knew that man does not live by bread alone. Freddie knew that his Father would provide for him.

He could not sacrifice his witness for mere cash.

Since then, Fred has been working with a Christian ministry reaching to the lost. Here is a poem Fred shared with me:

> *As the grass grows, as the wind blows,*
> *As the sun and the clouds, You really astound me.*
> *You're all around me, you're even inside me, too.*
> *You're always a friend, even after the end.*
> *Sweet Jesus, I know it's you,*
> *Sweet Jesus, I know it's you.*

They'll know
we are Christians by our love

As I write this, prominent God-fearing Christian teachers are denouncing each other once again — declaring that top leaders have been seduced by Hindu mysticism, Babylonian occultism and New Age neo-sorcery.

How should you or I respond?

Just as mothers did during the Civil War. Across such border states as Maryland, Tennessee and Missouri, families were divided as sons and fathers went to fight for the Union or the Confederacy. But the mothers saw no sense in it. Slavery, states' rights and regional pride faded in importance at the idea of brothers shooting at brothers.

Fathers were killing sons — just as we are doing today!

Mothers and wives stayed at home weeping and praying. Sometimes, they, too marched into battle — demanding that their little boys give up this foolishness.

So must we, for that's what we have today. *Christian civil war.*

It's time to demand that our brothers quit shooting at each other. But, they'll retort: *our cause is right, holy and noble!*

The combatants cite such evidence as symbols in fellow Christians' letterheads — rainbows, pyramids and stars, for example — use of methods shared by the world, and erroneous counseling techniques. *You've heard the denunciations.* You've read the bestselling Christian books that denounce this ministry or that charity.

All this has brought a fiery response from other Christian figures — particularly the ones denounced. They accuse their accusers of a lack of love, a poor understanding of grace, a de-

nial of miracles and Pharisee-like legalism. Many of the
Christian combatants seem indignant, if not furious, over the
other side's views of faith, the supernatural and interpretations of end-time prophecy.

They spend precious time bickering over such concepts as
the rapture, speaking in tongues, the tribulation, post-
millenialism, prosperity, visualization, and dominionism.

Such nitpicking divides our ever-arguing brotherhood to the
point that excellent teachers refuse to even appear on the
same platform with each other — or to have their words
printed in the same magazines. How can this go on while the
unchristian world watches and laughs? Whatever happened to
the joyous refrain: "And they'll know we are Christians by our
LOVE"?

I believe the arguing, finger-pointing, denouncing and accusing are a satanic strategy to keep us at each others'
throats — despite our love for and commitment to Jesus
Christ and one another. *The demonic goal?* To waste our time.
To put our eyes on one another instead of our Lord. To keep
us too busy to be fighting spiritual battles or building hedges
of thorns and walls of fire against demon forces!

To keep us away from the important task of working together to evangelize our neighborhoods, our nations and the
world for Christ.

Hell's demons must clutch their sides in hilarity as the
news media details the Church's latest "holy war." They must
howl in delight as prominent TV evangelists take valuable air
time to denounce each other in theological detail. They must
roll, laughing, in hell's aisles as one more book is printed that
fills believers with fear of fellow Christians. Our Church's corruption is very real. It's not particularly new. Look at what
John wrote to the early Church:

> *"Dearly beloved friends, don't always believe everything
> you hear just because someone says it is a message from
> God: test it first to see if it really is. For there are many
> false teachers around" (I John 4:1).*

So, yes, we've had problems throughout the ages. It seems
that the Apostle Paul encountered nothing but trouble as he
visited the early churches. He spent most of his time putting

out theological grassfires started by every would-be religious superstar. Problems continued through history. The Middle Ages' inquisitions against the Jews were not our faith's finest hour — nor were the conquests of the New World where natives were forced to "convert" at sword-point.

But now we have something new — but which we were warned was coming: This name-calling threatens our ability to obey the Great Commission. Accusers and counteraccusers weep publicly and quote II Peter 2:1-3:

"[False teachers] will cleverly tell their lies about God ... Many will follow their evil teaching that there is nothing wrong with sexual sin. And because of them, Christ and his way will be scoffed at. These teachers in their greed will tell you anything to get hold of your money...."

So, what shall you or I do? Do you begin denouncing the Church's denouncers one-by-one? Shall we turn this book into a *Holy Yellow Pages* of the good, the bad and the unrighteously ugly? Should I list preachers, ministries and charities I deem worthy of the Nicky Cruz Good Faithkeeping Seal of Approval ... then follow up with a blacklist of Evil Agents of the Antichrist? It certainly would make titillating reading. Perhaps I could rate this ministry or that. The XYZ Evangelistic Outreach gets 4 stars for theological correctness, but 5 pitchforks for sending money to somebody on my hitlist.

Some readers would love it, if past best-sellers are any indication.

Rather than having to depend on their own discernment, or on their personal study of the Word, or on the Lord's guidance — some Christians would rather have some highly persuasive author do their witch-hunting for them.

It's so convenient to have a list which says this charity is pure, but that one is wicked, or this ministry once used a New Age term in a pamphlet and so is demonic. Or that this leader once appeared on a platform with a Moslem and must not receive another dollar of support. We have a whole segment of Christian publishing that cranks out Christian horror. Instead of printing terrifying novels, they publish "true" scare documentaries — itemizing this terrible threat and that horrible conspiracy ... this awful charity and that offending brother. Readers are filled with fear and dread and, yes, hatred for fellow Christians. Several such accusation-packed "directories" have been enormous money-makers. It's exciting to pick up a paperback that lists organizations and leaders who — according to the authors — are in league with Satan, whether as unwitting proxies, duped agents, or willing conspirators in shadowy political organizations plotting to rule Earth and thwart Jesus' final triumphal entry.

I pray I do not become similarly guilty in your eyes of attacking my Christian brothers as I fill these pages. I pray I will not seem to hold up any specific fellow teacher for ridicule or ruin. I intend to object to principles and practices — not persons. I even intend to go to extreme lengths to disguise some of the offenders so that you will consider only the evil, not the doer. Yes, I have been counseled that a book that accuses prominent leaders by name will sell much better than one that merely assails deep, deep corruption. I know of at least one Christian author who succumbed to that counsel when his book's first draft was considered only marginally marketable without juicy accusations. The rewritten version sold by the hundreds of thousands.

And he joined the ranks of the divisive offenders.

I grieve for fellow Christians who have hardened their hearts against brothers or sisters whom they believe to be in error. We see such callousness — such judgment! *Let us hate the sin, but love the sinner!*

Praise God that I have not been judged and thrown into outer darkness every time I have sinned. There is no denying that I was a party to some very terrible things before I found the Lord.

Even so, I have experienced the great hurt of being shunned by a fellow Christian just because his and my theology are different. It hurts not to be able to share with my fellow co-worker in the Lord just because he and I have a different outlook on such things as baptism, speaking in tongues or abortion.

Are such differences important enough that we should violate Jesus' command that there be no divisions among us? Are such disagreements so great that we're to ignore the stern warnings that a house divided will surely fall?

No. We must agree to disagree and get on about our Father's business! The divisions among us are merely a successful satanic strategy to keep us fragmented and ineffective. Here's what the Apostle Paul thought of the bickering Christians in Corinth:

> "... *When you are jealous of one another and divide up into quarreling groups, doesn't that prove you are still babies, wanting your own way? In fact, you are acting like people who don't belong to the Lord at all"* (1 Cor. 3:3b).

Let me make a prediction. This book is going to threaten certain Christians. They're going to respond by attacking me. They'll pick something that I can't deny, such as that I believe that God is still in the business of miracles.

They may criticize my teaching that we must put an end to the centuries of Christian-versus-Christian bickering. They may charge that I am of the devil for suggesting that good Christians should have anything to do with Christians who do such things as worship on Saturdays, venerate the Virgin Mary, speak in tongues, or join religious communities.

Well, let me tell you: the divided condition of the Church must be a matter of great pride to Satan. *I suspect he has great strongholds protecting his abomination.* It's so important to his master plan!

I plead with you to take your eyes off of men for just a moment. Put them on Jesus. Close your ears to devisive talk and turn only to the Word — God's inspired Scriptures. Read with me Luke 11:14-23.

> *Once, when Jesus cast out a demon from a man who couldn't speak, his voice returned to him. The crowd was excited and enthusiastic, but some of them said, "No wonder he can cast them out. He gets his power from Satan, the king of demons!" Others asked for something to happen in the sky to prove his claim of being the Messiah.*
>
> *He knew the thoughts of each them, so he said, "Any kingdom filled with civil war is doomed.*
>
> *"So is a home filled with argument and strife.*
>
> *"Therefore, if what you say is true, that Satan is fighting against himself by empowering me to cast out his demons, how can his kingdom survive? And if I am empowered by Satan, what about your own followers? For they cast out*

demons! Do you think this proves they are possessed by Satan? Ask them if you are right! But if I am casting out demons because of power from God, it proves that the Kingdom of God has arrived.

"For when Satan, strong and fully armed, guards his palace, it is safe—until someone stronger and better-armed attacks and overcomes him and strips him of his weapons and carries off his belongings.

"Anyone who is not for me is against me. If he isn't helping me, he is hurting my cause."

Understanding that passage doesn't require years of seminary training. It gives us a test by which to evaluate anyone accused of advancing Satan's cause.

1) Is the teaching or person or group causing civil war of Christian versus Christian?
2) Is it bringing new strife and anger into the Church?
3) Is it throwing Satan out of his strongholds — or advancing sinfulness and rebellion, for example by teaching that we can become little gods or that we can set our own rules?
4) Is it dedicated to Christ Jesus as the only way for you and I to make peace with God?
5) Does it deny that Jesus was God's Son?
6) Does it promote benign, pointless, neutral activities which do nothing to spread the Gospel — except to keep Christians busy and out of true spiritual warfare?

Satan is **serious** about his battle against us. Wielding his weapons of confusion, strife and false accusation, he's pitted us at each other's throats—causing us to actually believe one another to be evil agents of hell! He's even brought us to actual war against each other.

Look at Northern Ireland. Christians actively ambush, murder, wound, maim and vow death against Christians. Nearby England is officially Episcopalian. Southern Ireland is officially Roman Catholic.

An English king centuries ago attempted to secure his battle gains in north Ireland by importing English Episcopalians and Presbyterian Scotsmen to live in Ireland's northernmost province of Ulster. Their arrival was met with angry bloodshed as indignation mixed violently with national pride and religious zealotry. The Catholics vowed to rid their island of heretics and rebels to the pope's authority. The Protestants swore to kill all "papists," whom they declared were disloyal to the crown and were agents of the Antichrist — deserving nothing better than burning at the stake.

Centuries later when Ireland won the right to choose independence from Great Britain, only the Protestant majority in Ulster voted to remain British. Radical Irish Catholics pledged to continue centuries-old efforts to throw them out — regardless that generations of Protestants had been born on Ulster soil and that the Presbyterians and Episcopalians were Irish natives now, too.

The war continues. There is no right side in the horrible murder spree. Key Protestant church leaders spew death threats and vows of murder just as loudly as their counterparts in the Irish Republican Army. The evil eye-for-an-eye war of never-ending vengeance wanes, then erupts, then settles down to random sniping murders instead of car bombs in front of schools or machine-gun extermination of entire families in their homes.

The only thing the two evil sides can agree upon is how much they hate peace groups which attempt to stop their fighting.

Are we that much different than these confused, deceived Christians of North Ireland? For centuries, they have hated one another and waged unending war — each pretending that they are doing God's bidding by ridding the earth of the other.

Meanwhile, Satan and his evil angels howl with mirth, delighted with all the souls dispatched to the Pit, delighted with the carnage, the hatred, the destruction and the shame brought to Jesus Christ.

But look at us. Are we any better? Not when we hate our Christian brothers!

What divides us? Frequently it is *nit-picking* **nonsense.** Do you know what divides three of America's largest brotherhoods of Bible-believing Christians? Theologically, the Churches of Christ, the Christian Churches (Disciples) and the Christian Churches/Churches of Christ (Independent) are virtually identical. What they teach is deeply founded in decades of dedicated study of the Bible.

But Satan has split these brotherhoods into warring camps over two incredible notions: first, that musical instruments should not be used in worship; and second, whether missionaries should raise their own support or be financed by a central outfit called the United Christian Missionary Society.

These three groups, all founded during the great Restoration Movement led by Alexander Campbell, shun each other.

What a tragedy! In many small towns across America, there will be a Catholic church, a Methodist church, a Presbyterian church, a Southern Baptist church, and three churches from this Restoration Movement.

Sometimes they war. Mostly they ignore each other — despite their common beliefs and roots. And you'll find that most fine Christians in all three churches have no idea what caused all the trouble ... nor who started the accusations.

Nor whether any of it is true.

The demon of the political arena

In a deep sleep, Michael suddenly found himself dreaming that he was in an enormous church auditorium. Up in the pulpit, his pastor was preaching away.

At the same time, the song leader was loudly doing his own thing — as were the choir director and the orchestra leader. The youth minister was telling jokes and going through his usual antics.

But nobody was paying particular attention to any of them. The entire congregation was doing its own thing — oblivious to anyone around them. Various people were giving special numbers amid the chaos, seemingly unaware of the hubbub. Others were giving hilarious testimonies, making stirring announcements or sharing great miracles in their lives.

Suddenly, Michael realized that up on the stage was the most hideous creature he'd ever seen — an enormously fat being that might have been a cross between an evil genie-in-a-bottle, a garden grub worm, and the *StarWars* movie character Jabba the Hutt.

Michael realized that the evil creature was the center of attention — no matter what everyone actually appeared to be doing. Indeed, members of the congregation were clawing and scrambling to get up to the gluttonous thing and present silver trays bearing offerings — which it grabbed and swallowed whole.

For brief moments, each church member received the thing's attention and approval. Then it would turn and gobble down the offerings of others climbing and shoving to get to the front.

As desperate people began handing up their children to the thing, Michael could stand no more.

"What are you?" he demanded. "Why are they doing this?" The thing turned its lazy eyes toward him.

"I'm the prince of the religious political arena," it answered. "They have come to worship me."

In his bed, Michael bolted awake.

He understood completely.

Shaken, he was convicted of his own sin — and the terrible condition of the Church in which he had been an elder for 15 years.

Yes, he had been guilty of lusting after the spotlight. He recounted the times he had been honored with a few moments in the pulpit to give a brief announcement or officiate a baby dedication.

He'd been consumed with making sure that he was a big hit — that what he said got a chuckle or else touched everyone's hearts *deeply*.

He thought of the many times that he had carefully glanced over at the pastor to be sure that the man was smiling his approval. And there were even those wonderful times when the preacher put his arm around Michael and his wife and — for all to hear — thanked the Lord for Michael's selfless sacrifices and deep humility.

Trembling, Michael thought about all the others in his church:

• The pastor who dared not preach about sin or self-denial, lest he jeopardize his own great popularity. Instead, he stroked the crowd with assurances that God loved them and wanted only prosperity for them.

• The church newsletter editor who carefully picked who would be featured in her monthly epistles — and who would be ignored. And whose prominently displayed column was designed to assert her own political importance.

• The church treasurer — who was actually the wife of the official treasurer — and how she carefully gripped the purse-strings, assuring her own status and guaranteeing a place of prominence for her husband.

• The leaders of the congregation's tiny and largely ineffective children's ministry — who were constantly seeking and receiving acclaim by the pastor, in whose best interest it was to present the impression that his church was an efficient, well-oiled machine worthy of the flock's tithes and offerings.

"Lord!" exclaimed Michael. "What must I do?"

"Examine your own motives," came the answer deep in his heart. "Are you serving yourself or Me?"

"Forgive me, Father," whispered Michael, glancing over at his sleeping wife. "Forgive me. What do I do?"

And Michael remembered a time from his teenage years. He'd been asked to sing an important solo in a church musical.

He'd practiced hard.

But as it came time to perform, he was convicted of his motives. He'd accepted the solo because it would put him in the spotlight. Everyone would applaud and say what a nice kid he was — and so talented!

"Lord," he had prayed, "blind their eyes to me. Let them see Jesus."

Filled with new strength and assurance, he had stepped up to the microphone.

Then, he let out a terrible squawk as he started off on the wrong note. Horribly, he stumbled up and down the musical scale, trying to get back onto the melody. He sang his part, then stepped back into the choir.

But he realized that no one was laughing at him.

Indeed, the congregation's faces were filled with praise and worship. They lifted up their hands, feeling the presence of their glorious and majestic God.

And Michael saw that the Lord had honored his prayer in a mighty way.

No one had heard his humiliating screeching. They had seen Jesus.

Now, in the night's darkness, "O, Lord," prayed Michael. "Renew me. Fill me once again with a desire to lift You up, not myself."

Evangelist Corrie ten Boom was that sort of selfless servant of the Lord. The Lord blessed her immensely. She never once solicited donations, yet she had all the free TV time she wanted. She was welcome in thousands of pulpits. A popular movie — *The Hiding Place* — was made of her life and played

worldwide. Publishers rushed her every word into print. The
Lord blessed her because she was *faithful.* She obeyed the inspired words of the Apostle Paul to be content in whatever
state the Lord puts us.

She didn't let the fame and publicity corrupt her. She kept
her eyes on Jesus. As God blessed her ministry beyond her
wildest dreams, she remained just a humble watchmaker
from Holland who loved Jesus with all her heart.

She kept her eyes on Jesus.

Some put theirs on money. It fails them — although they
are steadfast in their determination to continue the ministry
of God's Word. Others are corrupted by the power of their national position, the applause of millions and the adoration of
believers.

That all fades. It does not bring happiness or success. It
only brings emptiness and a desire for more.

I should know. *I've had the fame and the applause.*

Soon after I came to Jesus, I went to Bible college in La
Puente, California. After I graduated, the first job I got was
in a restaurant in Oakland. I had a few months — five, to be
exact — and then I would be off with my new bride. So in the
meantime I got a job as a busboy. *That's right, a busboy!* I
cleaned tables, swept floors and washed dishes. The restaurant was one of the nicest eating places in Oakland, right on
Jack London Square.

People with money, and many celebrities, came there to
spend money like crazy and drink like fish. The atmosphere
was not exactly healthy, morally or spiritually, for a young,
immature Christian right out of Bible college.

It was certainly a challenge to everything I had learned
and called for every scrap of spiritual protection I could find. I
thank God that He was with me, because I knew this was
where He wanted me to be for a while, even though deep in
my heart I knew that He was calling me into a definite future
ministry.

I worked with another busboy also from Puerto Rico. Roberto was constantly watching me. Often he and I ate lunch
together in a side room after the main push at lunchtime was
over and we could have a little breather. One day as I was
thanking God for the food, Roberto started laughing.

"Why are you talking to yourself?" he asked.

I stopped in the middle of my prayer and I explained I was thankful for everything Jesus gave me, and so I thanked Him for food and everything else. I said I knew Jesus personally, that He was right there with us, and I made it clear I was very serious about my faith.

Roberto sat there stunned. I knew he had been making fun of me before. To him it had been a funny thought to have someone talking to someone who wasn't there. The idea that Jesus was there in the room shook him up. Roberto didn't know what to say.

Roberto continued to scrutinize my every move. Wherever I went in the restaurant, whatever I did, I could feel Roberto's eyes on me, and I knew he was thinking and wondering. I took Roberto to my heart in prayer, and I shared what I knew about Jesus whenever I had the chance. I told him about the old days of witchcraft and fear in Puerto Rico, and the gang days in New York, and what Christ had done for me — and was doing every day. Roberto looked and listened.

Only one week later Roberto came with me to church. At the close of the service, when the invitation was given to come forward and accept Christ, Roberto knelt at the altar and gave his life to the Savior.

That was just the beginning. Most Puerto Ricans have large families, and counting all his brothers and sisters there were at least 15 in Roberto's. Through Roberto's newfound faith, every last member of his family, including his grandfather and grandmother, accepted Jesus. Three days after Roberto's conversion I left my job as a busboy to begin my own ministry. At the same time, Roberto quit to enter Bible college. Today he is a minister of the Gospel, giving all his time and effort to bringing Jesus to others.

What a blessing Roberto brought me! No matter how unknown I was at the time, no matter how insignificant I might be in anyone's eyes — and to many of the people I served, I was just a robot, moving food and dishes — I knew I had done something eternally important. It didn't matter now what happened. Lives had been changed, and would be changed, for the Lord. I came to that job a plain, straight Christian who loved Jesus. I was in the right place at the right time, and I left at the right time. I began preaching in Spanish-speaking churches in the area and found many hearts hungry for the Word. There were tremendous numbers of sincere people who listened, as Roberto had, to my simple message of Jesus and His life and power.

The burden to share Him grew deeper within me. I became very happy in those years of growing and sharing. Little by little I changed from a nobody to a somebody — at least in the public's eyes. God opened door after door, and the name Nicky Cruz became one which people started talking about.

When you become a "personality" it is easy to forget how your work began. How do you keep yourself humble when you see your name all over a city like a movie star's? How do you make the right decision when someone does something wrong to you, or forgive when you don't feel like forgiving? *These are questions I never find easy to answer.*

Prayer is constantly needed so we don't fall into temptation and pride. It is so easy to lose the burden God gave you, to lose sight of your calling, to forget that the Lord has brought you so far. There is a deep need to come closer and closer to Jesus every day, and never to forget Him.

God has been faithful. I have such beautiful memories, as I think back, of all Jesus has done for me.

I think of all the friends who pray for me. I look for such people wherever I go.

They are part of my life.

Without them and Jesus I couldn't do a thing. I try not to forget these partners in my ministry and their love and prayers. People often ask me, "Nicky, how did you get to where you are today?" It has not been my doing. Whatever I have done is a tribute to Jesus and my partners in prayer. But I want to emphasize this: *While I was attending Bible college, I wanted to become a missionary in South America.* It seemed like the natural thing to do, and what God would have me do. I knew Spanish, I was Spanish, I came from a Latin American country, so what else could God want me to do?

I announced my conclusion to the dean of the school, the Rev. Estevan Camarillo, and I will always remember what he said:

"Nicky, the will of God is not always what we want, or even what we may be quite sure is right. The best way to fulfill the will of God in your life is to serve Him totally every day. God may want to send you to South America. He may want to keeep you right here in California. I have an idea that He has a great ministry ahead for you. But I learned long ago that the Lord's ways are greater than our ways, and often far different from anything we can think or dream. Let it be the center of your ambition to give Him all your energy each day of your life, and He will take you where He wants you to go."

How true I have found those words of that wise man of God. I have made it my ambition to serve God to the best of my ability every day, day by day, and moment by moment, and God has done for me more than I could ask or think

It is so easy to fail in this area. We tend to take our eyes off the sky and look at the mud below. No one should ever corrupt the value of the calling of God in his life. Neither should we limit it, or be tempted into fanaticism.

We must learn to know ourselves and to know God, and as we make serving Him every day the center of our ambitions, He takes care of the rest.

It is easy to dream of the green pastures on the other side of the fence. People write to me so often to the effect: "If only I didn't have this job (or this wife or husband or this problem) how I would love to serve the Lord as you are doing."

Brothers and sisters, don't corrupt your calling. God has put you where you are just as He led me years ago to work as a busboy. If I hadn't been true to Him there, none of the other wonderful things that followed would have happened.

Roberto wouldn't be bringing men and women and boy and girls to Jesus today, and so many opportunities for God would have gone right down the drain.

Obey and you will see amazing things.

I can tell you all sorts of stories about witnessing in boldness and in the power of the Holy Spirit. How about Christian kids who hand out tracts outside of rock concerts? I've seen how effective that ministry can be — but only when the witnessing team seeks the Lord beforehand to lead them to the lonely, the hurting, the empty and the desperate that such concerts draw — and when they are obedient to His directing to talk to this one or give a tract to that one — even if he does have green hair or a skull and crossbones tattooed on his forehead.

How about the housewife who tackles the tough challenge of winning over the Mormons and Jehovah's Witnesses who knock on her door every two weeks? Listen, if you have a burden for those folks, you'd better get on your knees before you jump into the battle unarmed. Those folks know how to fight back.

They can plant such confusion and doubt in your heart that you're scared to try again. But with the Lord's calm assurance that this is, indeed, His way for you, and with His anointing on your weeks of Bible study, prayer and fasting ... you can do it. Quite a few turned-on Christians have been rescued out of those two cults.

Go for it. But do it in His power.

Listening for His direction.

Obey His true voice and you've got some amazing adventures ahead of you.

Such as ministering to pagan natives.

Or drugged-out street kids.

Or witches. Yes. Witches.

They're growing in number. They are not to be feared. But they're headed straight to hell — and are taking deceived people with them.

With God's help, you can be the one who keeps Lucifer from having a few more witches with whom to spend a horrible eternity.

But only go in God's strength.

Into the evil darkness

Have you ever met a good witch? In the Third World, witches and sorcerers are quite common — and are not merely something on Saturday morning children's television.

There are over 100 million followers of spiritism worldwide, reports Andreas Resch, director of the Institute for Para-Science in Austria. He says the center of spiritism is in Brazil, where there are 11 million followers. Great Britain is second, and there has been a sharp increase in interest throughout West Germany. There, the Bishops Conference of the United Protestant-Lutheran Church recently issued sharp warnings against the occult. God has given us clear guidelines, too.

"He will guide you into all truth ... and he will show you things to come" (John 16:13 King James Version).

Just what does that verse mean?

It means that only God is permitted to let you or me peek ahead into the future. He has allowed only a few prophets and other men of God this privilege. If we get tired of waiting for God to show us the future and decide to seek such secrets from the forces of evil, we get ourselves into big trouble. That is, if we don't care to follow God's way, there is only one alternative: Satan's. And believe this — he is the author of everything involved in the occult. I t is not an innocent pastime.

It is never good. Caribbean voodoo queens, South African witch doctors and Central American caciques often claim to be good. But they are not. They wield enormous, evil power over the masses. In Europe, their brothers talk of being the true, "old religion" and paint nostalgic word pictures of kindly Druids and life-giving keepers of nature. In the emerald forests of South America, they pretend to protect the indigenous civilization of noble savages untainted by the white man's religion. In civilized Japan and Burma and India, they lift up prayers, incense and offerings to demon-faced images whom the populace fears and reveres. And in civilized America, some offer palm readings, astrological readings and spiritual counsel — frequently amid much pretense they are Christians. But, there is no such thing as a "white witch" — despite what you may hear from the false prophets of weekday mid-morning TV.

"Good witches" resist the cause of Christ. They are jealous of the great power of His holy Name. They know that they wield only deception and darkness from Satan. And in the final battle, they know, they are doomed to complete defeat.

West German evangelist Reinhardt Bonnke took an enormous revival tent to South Africa. There, local witches and witch doctors began putting curses on his revival — after they heard of the tens of thousands healed and saved at other Bonnke meetings elsewhere in Africa.

They called on demonic powers to destroy the tent—which was the largest canvas structure in the world. And sure enough, one night, a powerful wind came up and shreaded it.

The witch-doctors' glee made all the newspapers in South Africa as they danced around the remains, took credit for the destruction and boasted their power over the white man's God.

But our great Creator is not mocked. He is far more powerful than Satan's snarling rebels. So, upon the urging of the Holy Spirit, local organizers and Bonnke knew they were to hold the revival anyway. They knew *Jehovah Jireh*—our provider—would provide a new tent.

So, tens of thousands gathered under the skeletal cables of the tent's remains. And despite cold winds and chilling rain all around the area, attendees at the revival remained warm and dry — protected from the elements by a mighty *spiritual* umbrella.

That's right! To hear the Bonnke people tell about it, local intercessors continued to ask the Lord to honor their months of hard work to prepare for the Bonnke revival and their months of prayer that thousands would come to know the Lord at the meetings. And He was faithful. *He is not defeated by the worst that hell offers.*

Are we to fear the forces of darkness? Never. But, a little healthy respect doesn't hurt. It's good to know your enemy. I rode on an airplane with a witch who was a very talkative, 50ish woman on a flight from Denver to Cleveland.

She asked me why I was flying. I told her about meetings I was going to attend — then mentioned books I had written.

I brought up *Run, Baby, Run* and *Satan on the Loose* —which I noted was about witchcraft. Suddenly, she was very interested. "That's my topic!" she exclaimed. "By the way, I have a problem because people call me a witch. Three times I have cursed people and everything I said came true." She began to detail all the occult experiences she'd had. She bragged to me that one man had dropped dead after she cursed him for mistreating her. Another curse had been put on a large store when she took a dislike to a man affiliated with it. She told me that she cursed the place so that it would be destroyed in two months.

Sure enough, she bragged, it was destroyed well within the time limit and the man was reduced to poverty. I was astonished at how everything she said revealed incredible selfishness. The third curse had been put on a restaurant when they failed to serve her the lobsters she had ordered. She cursed it to burn down to nothing — and it did only days later.

I began to pray. The Lord told me not to witness to her. She had been sent to disturb me and thwart my witness. She was completely Satan's. I looked at her and spoke softly to the evil one inside her, "I know you and from where you come. You do not intimidate me, Satan. I am going to do what I have been called to do. I am going to terrorize your territory with the power of God. With the resurrection of Jesus. With all the billions of angels. We are going to blast every form of evil that you use to come to deceive, destroy or to build up your kingdom."

Politely, then, I said goodbye to the woman. As you might guess, she had very little else to say to me on that flight.

I closed my eyes and remembered why I wrote my book *Satan on the Loose*. It had been impressed on me that one of the most corrupting forces in the world today is the occult.

Fascination with this dark side of the supernatural is sweeping through every country and every area of life. Once such interest was limited to $5 fortune-tellers in back alleys and to seances in small, dark rooms where desperately searching men and women tried to make contact with someone they had lost in death. Not anymore! Today the occult is big business. Books, movies, games, schools — everyone seems to be trying to cash in on the tremendous interest in the supernatural.

What a tragedy!

What a mission field for us!

What a challenge for the prayer warrior, too. America was founded as a Christian nation. We cannot sit idly by and let the enemy steal what is not his!

The plague in our midst

I was stunned when former Secretary of the Treasury and White House official Donald Regan disclosed one of the serious complications he'd had in getting anything accomplished in the Ronald Reagan administration: *Nancy's obsession with astrology.*

"Virtually every major move and decision the Reagans made during my time as White House Chief of Staff was cleared in advance with a woman in San Francisco who drew up horoscopes to make certain that the planets were in a favorable alignment for the enterprise," he wrote in his book, *For the Record.*

What a terrible blow to the cause of Christ! I believe that this revelation about Mrs. Reagan has given more positive publicity to the forces of darkness than any news in centuries. She fought such a good fight, too, in her battle against drugs. I wish she had just said "No," to the astrologers! Instead, I believe Satan has used her to bring about a revival of witchcraft and the occult in the United States unlike anything we've yet seen.

What an irony, too. President Reagan had been champion for many Christian causes — prayer in schools, the banning of abortion, legalization of creationism, to name a few.

But now we learn that since the late 1940s, Nancy had been deep into this ancient evil that teaches the planets determine our fate. It was fear of the stars that dictated Reagan's eccentric inauguration as Governor of California at 12:10 a.m. — ten minutes after midnight.

As Don Regan's book hit the streets, we learned that Nan-

cy's astrology delvings were a carefully guarded secret which
had nevertheless leaked out several times — including in
1980 when the President admitted consulting fortune-teller
Jeane Dixon. A delegation from the Federation of American
Scientists — including five Nobel Prize winners — then wrote
to Reagan, protesting that they were "gravely disturbed" by
his admission of meeting with Dixon as well as the disclosure
that he read his horoscope daily.

"In our opinion, no person whose decisions are based, even
in part, on such evident fantasies can be trusted to make the
many serious — and even life-and-death — decisions required
of American Presidents," the scientists protested in their
letter.

President Reagan himself supposedly didn't take the star
readings all that seriously until his assassination attempt by
John Hinckley. Then, on Nancy's urging, an astrologer was
consulted constantly. Don Regan wrote that he was forced to
maintain a color-coded desk calendar to keep track of the
Chief Executive's "good," "bad" and "be careful" days. There
were frequent days when strict adherence to the horoscope
forced the cancellation of meetings and restriction of activities
in the White House. The 1985 summit with the Soviet Union
was planned carefully with an eye on Reagan's horoscope
readings, according to Regan's book.

In the weeks after its release, newspapers were full of in-
terviews with astrologers. Magazines and supermarket tabloids took a new interest at this "interesting phenomenon."
They all asked, "Does it work?" In unison, all the mediums
and chart-makers and New Agers chorused, "YES!"

New books on the joys of the occult flooded the newsstands.
On an airplane flight between Tucson and Dallas I sat next to
a woman who was reading up on astrology. When she saw me
glance at her book she said, "You look like a Capricorn."

"You're right," I said, "but I have something better than astrology." Then I told her that I don't need to find out what influences the stars may have on my life, for I know the One
who holds the stars in the hollow of His hand.

This lady looked very uncomfortable as I talked about Jesus. I've found truth so often in what Paul said:

"Don't be teamed with those who do not love the Lord, for

what do the people of God have in common with people of sin? How can light live with darkness? What harmony can there be between Christ and the devil?" (II Cor. 6:14, 15).

It is here that we have to be so careful! The devil loves to twist this truth and cause such dissention between Christian brothers! Of course we cannot ignore this verse.

We *must* be on guard. America was founded by godly men. Just read the writings of Christopher Columbus, George Washington and Abraham Lincoln and you'll see where they got their strength.

Today there are godly politicians. Who? Well, believe it of not, Pat Robertson is not the only office seeker who believes in God and embraces Jesus as Lord. The Congress is full of Christians.

And here's a fine Christian lawmaker that you may not even know about. Great Britain's Prime Minister Margaret Thatcher. That's right, England's Iron Maiden — credited with returning the United Kingdom to prosperity and hope — freely espouses Christ.

Here's an excerpt from one of her remarkable public speeches, which, of course, never made it into America's press:

"...The Old Testament lays down in Exodus the Ten Commandments as given to Moses, the injunction in Leviticus to love our neighbor as ourselves and generally the importance of observing a strict code of the law.

"The New Testament is a record of the Incarnation, the teachings of Christ and the establishment of the Kingdom of God. Again we have the emphasis on loving our neighbor as ourselves and to 'Do-as-you-would-be-done-by.'

"I believe that by taking together these key elements from the Old and New Testaments we gain a view of the universe, a proper attitude to work and principles to shape economic and social life.

"We are told we must work and use our talents to create wealth. 'If a man will not work, he shall not eat,' wrote St. Paul to the Thessalonians. Indeed, abundance rather than poverty has a legitimacy which derives from the nature of Creation.

"Nevertheless, the Tenth Commandment — Thou shalt not covet — recognizes that making money and owning things could become selfish activities. But it is not the crea-

*tion of wealth that is wrong, but love of money for its own
sake.*

*"The spiritual dimension comes in deciding what one
does with the wealth. How could we respond to the many
calls for help, or invest for the future, or support the wonderful artists and craftsmen whose work also glorifies God
unless we had first worked hard and used our talents to
create the necessary wealth? "*

Amazing words for a politician. Yet, Mrs. Thatcher talks like
this all the time. Sure, she is criticized. But, those who follow
British politics know that she could care less. She has an inner
strength that Nancy Reagan would do well to study — rather
than dabbling in forbidden dark arts.

I've been impressed with how great the gulf is between
Christ and Satan — and how sharply we have to draw the
line if we're going to be on the side of God and Christ.

Lois Hoadley Dick of Newton, New Jersey, has told of her
friend Janet who visited a gathering of spiritualists. Terribly
depressed when she arrived and sorry she had come, Janet
started repeating to herself the promises of I John 1:7, *"... the
blood of Jesus Christ his Son cleanseth us from all sin."*

The leader tried several times to begin the seance, without
success. Finally he announced, "There is someone here who is
hindering the service. I cannot do anything until you leave."
So Janet got up and walked out. She realized she had come to
a place where she had no right to be, and apparently the spiritualists could not coexist with the blood of Christ.

Twenty years ago, the movie *The Exorcist* was a shocking
portrayal of the satanic possession of a 12-year-old girl. The
film opened the door to a whole genre of similar motion pictures filled with gore.

The language and actions of the young heroine of *The Exorcist* became unspeakably repulsive on the screen as the devil
took control of her mind and body.

I need not detail the long list of similar movies that have
followed. But an explosion of the occult followed. Moviegoers
seemingly loved being scared speechless by demons, devils,
murdering cultists and other such stuff of which nightmares
are made. The craze moved to Saturday morning cartoons.

And increasingly, our generation is fascinated with the supernatural — largely because of the careful indoctrination that the TV generation has had in matters of witchcraft and sorcery. One result is that Christians in the United States absolutely hate to deal with the fact that magic, sorcery and non-Christian mysticism can NOT be accepted as fascinating, funny, exciting and perfectly acceptable entertainment.

Magic is wrong, even if it's only in a classic Disney movie, a traditional Halloween TV special, reruns of "harmless" *Bewitched* or *I Dream of Jeannie,* or a Steven Spielberg extraterrestrial Oscar-winner! It's particularly terrible in children's Saturday morning and after-school "super-hero" cartoons.

The Bible absolutely prohibits supernatural skill that doesn't come from Almighty God. Yet, we leave our kids with a babysitting TV that instructs them in the thrill and excitement of dabbling with the dark side! Friends, it is a lie that we can better stimulate our Christian children's imaginations and creativity by filling their minds with magical worlds. There is no place in the Christian home for bumbling wizards and brave Ghostbusters, good witches and heavenly Care Bears, Dungeons and Dragons, blue fairies, pet monsters, funny teen werewolves, friendly ghosts or benevolent Papa Smurfs.

As unsettling as it may seem, we must reexamine our favorite movies for kids: *The Wizard of Oz,* complete with good and bad witches; the Disney greats with their kindly fairy godmothers; and the new Lucas and Spielberg classics with supernatural gremlins and "truth-bearing" extra-terrestrials.

Don't offer your kids on the altar of television! I never cease to be astonished by parents who will leave their youngsters in front of such a foul-mouthed, death-spewing babysitter. If the teenage girl next door taught your youngsters how to conjure up evil spirits, talk to the dead and use "good" magic — as on such cartoon fare as *Dungeons and Dragons,* the *Care Bears, Rainbow Bright, Masters of the Universe* and the *Smurfs,* you probably would ban her from your home. Yet the first household luxury to be repaired when it goes on the fritz is the TV. The dishwasher can wait. The toaster can, too. And the garbage disposal.

But not the TV. It keeps the kids happy.

Transfixed, they stare into its hypnotic eye and learn all about a mystical world where there is no God, no Jesus, no Holy Spirit — just wonderful spirits and sprites and friendly monsters who giggle out the cutest little incantations to get what they want.

The occult world is many-headed, and every head sprouts from a single source — Satan.

Don't fool around with magic, astrology, reincarnation, gurus, spiritualism, inner visions, mystic auras, astral travel, Ouija, witchcraft, or anything of the kind. All of it is from below, not from above — from the devil, not from God.

Ban it from your home. Rid your personal library of books about witches and sorcery and magical spells. Turn off the TV.

Spend time with your kids. That may not be easy at first. So, I suggest that you sit down and watch cartoons with them. You will be repulsed by what you'll see. You may weep.

A generation is being raised on this demonic garbage.

I'm conscious as never before of the way the forces of evil are lined up against the powers of God. I predict that in the days ahead, occultism will enter more and more of our whole society. The stage is being set. People have turned from God to science to solve their problems. Now, with the increasing uncertainty of our economy, with our scientific achievements threatening to destroy us, we are realizing that science can't solve all our problems either.

Earlier in this book, I spoke of witches fasting and praying in order to bring about the fall of the Christian world — and particularly the family life of our Christian community. They were praying to Satan, also, that top evangelists would be disgraced and their families ruined. Since I was raised in the middle of Caribbean witchcraft — both of my parents were practicing witches in rural Puerto Rico — I know how this evil works through the mind.

In the movie StarWars, the forces of good and evil were portrayed as light and dark. That's a little simplistic. Actually, the very worst evil can portray itself as magnificent goodness and light.

Strange occult forces beckon.

I believe they will continue to trap many more victims. Don't let them trap you! I have a favorite little story that I believe makes my point.

Once upon a time, a cat smiled its most winning smile at a bird. "What lovely feathers you have," it purred. "How beautiful they are — particularly those long, pretty ones on the tips of your wings."

"Oh, yes," chirped the foolish bird. "They certainly are gorgeous."

"I am so envious," purred the cat. "I am just an ugly cat who will never fly in the air so gracefully as you."

"Yes, yes," agreed the bird. "I do fly so gracefully."

"Purrrrrrhaps," whispered the cat, "you would take pity on me. I would *purrrrhaps* find contentment down here on the ground if you would be so kind to give me some of your beautiful feathers."

"Certainly, certainly," chirped the bird, plucking out the most beautiful ones. And all morning, as the cat purred her most eloquent flatteries, the bird strutted back and forth, plucking out its feathers and giving them to the oh-so-grateful cat.

Around noon, the cat stood, stretched her claws and began grinning at the bird hungrily. Alarmed, the bird spread her wings and realized that — Agh! — she was completely naked.

But it was too late. The cat pounced, scattering all the feathers for which she really had no use at all.

She had been after something else altogether.

Just a bit fatter that afternoon, the cat spoke to a plump robin:

"My, what lovely feathers you have ..."

Brothers, and sisters, do not be seduced.

Do not trade your holiness for the compromises that the world suggests.

"Take no part in the worthless pleasures of evil and darkness, but instead rebuke and expose them," warns Ephesians 5:11.

Well, just how do we rebuke and expose them?

How to
fight back

So, how do mere Christians wage war against the Prince of Darkness? A good friend of mine, Bobby Cruz, is the pastor of the growing House of Worship in Miami. As I write this, attendence runs around 2,000 each Sunday.

Bobby — who is not related to me, except as a Christian brother and former street gang member in New York City — has a powerful ministry in Miami among people trapped in a terrible cult called Santeria. Perhaps you remember the Hollywood movie about it *The Believers,* which included a scene in which a small boy was killed and offered on a satanic altar as a human sacrifice.

The cult is real and terrible, says Bobby. It's been called a Cuban form of voodoo, but it's actually much worse than that. It's a demonic corruption of Roman Catholicism. People caught up in Santeria believe that the saints will protect them if offered sacrifices and if their statues are venerated in bizarre ways. Some of these people have life-sized statues filling their homes, all surrounded by special foods and other offerings.

What does Bobby do to prepare himself to do battle against Santeria?

"A soldier has to be ready at all times — and ready to die, too," he says. "You've got to know who your enemy is. And you've got to know the Word." Additionally, Bobby's church has a 24-hour prayer network. More than 100 people participate each week, ensuring that several members are interceding for their pastor around the clock.

More than 100 people a month come to the Lord through

Bobby's ministry. Many of them have been rescued from Santeria.

"It's a religion of fear," he says. "They believe that if they leave Santeria, the saints will punish them. They believe that if they get rid of their statues — which are usually covered with gold and jewels — that the saints will get them.

"When we minister to them, we don't come against Santeria. We ask if they believe in Jesus.

"Of course, they do.

"So, I ask if Jesus is stronger than the saints.

"He is, they agree. Can the saints conquer Jesus? No, of course not, they tell me. Well, I tell them, put your trust in Jesus and He'll protect you against the saints!"

Of course, converts grow in the Lord and usually become quite vocal in expressing how silly their superstition was. But for those still in Santeria, it is serious stuff. So, using the prophet Elijah as a model, Bobby mocks the saints, just like Elijah mocked the prophets of Baal.

"A while back, this lady brought me her two statues in a sack for me to destroy for her," remembers Bobby. "She told me not to touch them — that she was scared for my safety if I touched them. So, I looked in and grabbed one in each hand. I held them up and asked. 'Which one didn't you want me to touch, this one or this one?' She almost fainted. So, I banged one against the desk and it shattered. 'Hmmmmm,' I said. 'I still feel OK. Let's see what happens to me if I knock this one's head off."

He did just that. And as the horror-stricken woman stared, no lightning bolts struck Bobby. He didn't fall over dead. He didn't break out in boils. He just dusted off his hands and asked if she had any more Santeria idols.

"I wouldn't even begin to do things like that if I didn't have people praying for me and if I wasn't keeping my own life straight — in the Word and in prayer."

Bobby's quite a warrior. I like to call him my spiritual son, although we're quite close in age. He and his friend Richie Ray may be familiar to any reader who likes Latin *salsa* music. Not so many years ago, the two of them had a number of top hits.

When they came to know Jesus, they brought their unique style of music with them — something you'll just have to experience for yourself should you visit their congregation in Miami.

They've used their voices and guitars and keyboards as mighty weapons against the devil.

I have another weapon. Righteous anger.

I know what the devil did to my family. For centuries we lived under a terrible curse. My father and mother practiced witchcraft. I grew up with people coming to them to be healed and to curse other people. I know what a terrible, real entity Satan is. He is my blood enemy. And he hates me.

Through the blood of Jesus, I broke his grip on my family.

I know how bad he is.

And I know how to defeat him.

Satan: Don't believe anything good about him

A lot of people get uptight if you mention Satan. That name may bring a mental picture of someone with horns, a tail, and a pitchfork.

But I'm not talking about a fantasy. *The devil is a reality.*

To understand him, you've got to go back to the beginning. Bible passages show Satan was one of the highest and most beautiful angels in Heaven. He was close to God. He must have wanted to be bigger than God. And at some point before the earth was created, Satan swelled with pride. He conspired with other angels to try to overthrow God and take His throne.

Naturally, the plot failed.

When God saw the wicked pride in this powerful being, He cast him and the other evil angels clear out of heaven.

God had created the angels to serve Him — and they were given a free will. Apparently, however, none have ever challenged God's authority before. While we don't know enormous details about heavenly history, the Bible does give us little tidbits, such as:

• Lucifer had been the guardian of the Throne of the Most High and was called the light-bearer and son of the morning.

• He may have been the highest in authority over all the other angels, second only to God.

• He invented sin. That's somewhat difficult to understand until you see that no angel had ever chosen to defy the great Creator. It was sheer folly — for what chance could the lowly creations have against the all-powerful, all-knowing, all-present Creator of all? However, Lucifer was envious of God. Isaiah says of him:

> *"How you are fallen from heaven, O Lucifer, son of the morning! How you are cut down to the ground— mighty though you were against the nations of the world. For you said to yourself: 'I will ascend to heaven and rule the angels. I will take the highest throne. I will preside on the Mount of Assembly far away in the north. I will climb to the highest heavens and be like the Most High.' But instead, you will be brought down to the pit of hell, down to its lowest depths. Everyone there will stare at you and ask, 'Can this be the one who shook the earth and the kingdoms of the world? Can this be the one who destroyed the world and made it into a shambles and demolished its greatest cities and had no mercy on his prisoners?' " (Isaiah. 14:12-17)*

• His rebellion — joined by legions of other angels — was turned back by God's faithful angels, led by the warrior archangel Michael. The rebels were banished from Heaven and condemned to hell at the end of time, where they would be punished for all eternity.

• Immediately upon man's creation, Lucifer sought new vengeance against God — and spread his rebellion to this new creature. He deceived man with lies, persuading Eve that if she disobeyed God's one rule — not to eat from the Tree of Knowledge of Good and Evil — she would become just as wise as the Lord.

• Ever since, Lucifer and his rebels have endeavored to corrupt and ruin man's relationship with God — spreading ridiculous lies about the Most High, among them fashioning alternative ways to heaven, which won't work, but will cause men to waste their years on Earth before being condemned to hell.

One excellent proof of his existance today is his earnest public relations campaign. He is filled with ugly pride and he wants us to think that he's gotten a bad name unjustly — and that we should follow him instead of God. He's even managed to infest quite a number of philosophies with a completely different view of his nature and origin.

For example, look at what groups as seemingly wholesome as the Masonic Lodge, Shriners, Eastern Star, Rainbow Girls and DeMolay boys teach about Satan. James D. Shaw, a former 33rd degree Mason and the author of *The Deadly Deception*, published by Huntington House, writes that the Masonic Lodge believes that Satan is real, but is not an enemy of God, seeking to tempt, deceive and destroy — mankind has merely "supposed" this.

The truth is, Masons are taught, Lucifer, the "Light Bearer" is actually good and the instrument of liberty. He is generally *misunderstood and maligned*, according to Masonic teaching. Shaw quotes a number of Masonic texts such as *Morals and Dogma* by Albert Pike. In the section for instructing Masons studying for the third degree, this handbook teaches:

> *"The true name of Satan, the Kabalists say, is that of Yahweh reversed; for Satan is not a black god ... For the initates he is not a Person, but a Force, created for good, but which may serve for evil. It is the instrument of Liberty or Free Will.*

In the same book on page 321, the same text instructs those studying for the 19th degree:

> *"Lucifer, the Light-Bearer! Strange and mysterious name to give to the Spirit of Darkness! Lucifer, the Son of the Morning! Is it he who bears the Light, and with all its splendors intolerable, blinds feeble, sensual, or selfish Souls? Doubt it not!"*

Then, those achieving the 32nd degree are taught in the handbook:

> *"... there is no rebellious demon of Evil, or Principle of Darkness coexistent and in eternal controversy with God, or the Principal of Light...."*

Another group that takes an odd and unscriptural view of Satan is the Jehovah's Witnesses. They are taught that Jesus is not God at all, but that Jehovah had two sons, Lucifer and Michael. The latter briefly came to earth as a man called Jesus. Also, the Witnesses are taught, there is no hell and no devil.

The Church of Jesus Christ of Latter-Day Saints (Mormons) also teaches that Lucifer is Jesus' brother and is the "second-born creature of God after Jesus."

What does the Bible say about Satan?

Satan is the father of lies, accuser of the brethren, deceiver, tempter and ruler of the kingdom of darkness. He hates the one creation in God's image — Man. He blinds the lost to the glorious light of the Gospel, and seeks to be worshiped as he works to steal, kill and destroy.

He is the enemy we are to resist and the one Jesus came to defeat.

What will happen to him eventually? John, foreseeing the end of time, wrote in Revelation 12:9,10:

> *"And the great dragon was cast out, that old serpent, called the Devil, and Satan, which deceived the whole world: he was cast out into the earth, and his angels were cast out with him...the accuser of our brethren is cast down...."*

Thus, Satan has been condemned for centuries and knows that he will spend eternity in hell, tormented forever. As vengeance against God, he's vowed to take as many of us with him as he can.

He even tried to deceive Jesus and thus thwart God's sacrifice to forgive the sins of rebellious men:

> *"And Jesus being full of the Holy Ghost returned from Jordan, and was led by the Spirit into the wilderness, being forty days tempted of the devil..." (Luke 4:1,2)* .

However, we're given all sorts of promises that he can't really hurt us—if we obey God's instructions concerning him:

> *"Resist the devil and he will flee from you" (James 4:7).*

> *"Put on the whole armor of God, that you may be able to stand against the wiles of the devil...For we wrestle not against flesh and blood, but ... against the rulers of the darkness..." (Eph. 6:11,12).*

Deception and lies are his greatest tools.

> *"...the god of this world hath blinded the minds of them which believe not, lest the light of the glorious gospel of Christ...should shine unto them" (II Cor. 4:4).*

How do we fight back? When I was quite small, I can remember hoeing some weeds in my father's garden and thinking that I was doing a good job. I got rid of a whole row of weeds — at least I went down the row of beans and chopped off every weed in sight. When I got to the end of the row I stopped and looked back, pretty proud that all the weeds were gone. Then I noticed my father watching me. He came over to where I was leaning on my hoe and asked, "Are you finished, Nicky?"

"Sure!" I said. "Look, Father, the weeds are all gone!"

"No, Nicky," my father said. "Look."

He knelt down in the garden and poked his finger into the ground. "See this root? As long as you leave the roots, the weeds will deep growing. It's not enough to chop off the tops. You must cut deep into the ground and kill the roots if you want to keep the weeds from growing."

Roots. What about getting rid of corruption for good? *How about killing the root!*

Some people may think it just happens there are so many corrupters in the world. They think it is human nature or an accident that so many good things are spoiled by so may bad things — pride, greed, violence, and all the rest. I say that if you see many plants of a weed growing close together, you know they come from the same root. And if you see the same kinds of corruption spoiling things in every part of the world over hundreds of years, they must grow out of one root.

To put it another way, when a number of women in Boston were all strangled in the same way, the police concluded that the murders were all committed by the same person. They were — by the Boston Strangler. When people all over the world are destroyed morally and spiritually in the same basic way, sensible people should conclude that the destruction must come from one source. The Bible says that source is the devil — the biggest corrupter of all times.

How do we fight back? Holiness. Brothers and sisters, in part this is a book about unfaithful shepherds. But what I hope you take away with you now is a new yearning for the mind of Jesus Christ. **Holiness.** A love from Jesus that is unpretentious, wholesome and down-to-earth.

For as a holy people, no weapon that Satan can devise will ever touch us.

Even when he is trying his evil worst.

The evil need not touch you

At a freeway off-ramp in Colorado Springs, a little station wagon was getting ready to make a left turn as the driver waited for the signal to change.

When the light turned green, she took her foot off of the brake, stepped on the accelerator and entered the intersection just as she had hundreds of times before.

Then, suddenly, her world collapsed in a crash and a shower of exploding glass. Everything went black as a truck spun the shattered car around. The station wagon's driver slumped over the wheel, unconscious.

There was silence. Witnesses gasped at the terrible sight. "Dear God!" "Is she dead?" "Somebody get help — PLEASE!"

A young man tried to wrench open the station wagon's door. There was the strong smell of oil and gasoline. He knew he had to get her out of the car before it erupted into flames.

But the woman remained slumped, motionless over the wheel — her face a mass of blood and glass.

Thinking quickly, the young man recruited a bystander to help him rip out the sun roof. As they peered down at the woman, they realized she was having difficulty breathing. One of the young men held up her head cautiously.

I had been on the way to my office to sign some letters before catching a flight to a two-day speaking engagement. I was getting ready for a trip to Holland, where I intended to confront a large group of satanists that had contacted me. Worship of the devil is particularly blatant in the Netherlands — the seemingly peaceful land of windmills, tulips, dikes and Hans Brinker. At the driver's wheel, my ministry's executive director, John

Arana, suddenly slowed. "Nicky," he said, "that looks like a bad, ugly accident."

I nodded. "It looks pretty bad."

As we neared, I peered at the crumpled little car. Then, the stunning reality hit me.

That was *my* car!

That was Gloria. My wife. My best friend. My only real confidant on Earth. For a fleeting moment, I dared not believe that she was still alive.

"Please, God," I prayed, "don't let her suffer."

John saw, too. He stopped the car.

But I was already out of the car and running to the wreck. The young man on the roof asked who I was as I gently reached in to touch my beloved.

"That's my wife," I answered. I took her head in my hands and began to think and pray. Everything within me, my emotions, my sense of time, my awareness of what was going on around us, seemed to be frozen. I just could not believe that my wife was sitting there hopeless — blood oozing from her face, her mouth, her hands. My heart cried out as I began to beseech the Lord to preserve her life.

Just minutes before she had pulled out of our family driveway to take our daughter, Elena, to school.

"Goodbye," Gloria had said as she gave me a kiss, "I'll see you in two days. Have a good crusade."

Now she lay crushed, pinned in the twisted metal, unconscious — dying for all I knew. Deep feelings of pain and sorrow such as I'd never felt before swept through me. This was the one woman that I loved. The mother of my children. My best friend. My love. My moral support. My emotional stability in times of trouble. Broken. Bloody. In great pain. Then I began to hear a moaning. She was trying to assure me that she was OK. But she could not talk. She hurt. But she was trying to be strong.

Wasn't that just like her? Trying to help me when it was she who was in agony. In a whisper, I prayed over her. And I could tell that she could recognize my voice. My heart leaped within me for joy.

I had seen blood before.

Many times.

As a street kid, I had held my best friend, Manny, in my arms as
he clutched onto life. It had been snowing. The sky was grey. I
was on my knees, hugging Manny to my chest, rocking back and
forth in despair, knowing the ambulance would not arrive in
time. As the blood from his 32 switchblade stab wounds soaked
the ground about us, he breathed a deep sigh — then no more. I
had been filled with intense anger. I would avenge him. I would
kill those who had killed him.

I screamed aloud to the cold, grey sky. Why had God allowed
Manny to die? If there was a God, He wasn't my friend. I certain-
ly wasn't interested in Him. I had never believed in Him any-
how. Kneeling in the bloody snow, I had nowhere to turn. I was
at an emotional, psychological, physical and spiritual dead end.

But this wasn't Manny. This was my beloved Gloria. And I
was no longer that restless young lion, the rebel without a
cause, searching the skies for answers or solutions. Now I had
the Lord Jesus Christ with me.

As I held her head gently and watched her pain, I wanted so
much to embrace her and convey to her my love and support.
But I couldn't. I had to hold her head steady in my hands. I had
to protect her neck.

Otherwise, she might be paralyzed.

In the midst of this rush of emotion, I hoped and prayed that
there was no danger of that. I could see that her leg had been
shattered. There was no way I could move her since the metal
pinned her to the seat. *At that moment, I realized how much dif-*
ferent this situation was from Manny's death. Now, I was not in
defiance of God. This time, He was my friend. The Creator of the
universe — on Whom I could call.

And Gloria knew Him, too. *Unlike Manny, she was filled with*
faith. A faith strengthened by hours of intercession and years of
trusting dependence on Him.

I whispered a prayer and had an unusual sense of the
Holy Spirit's presence. I glanced around and saw John torn
apart in tears. That stunned me. As desperate and confused as I
was by the accident, I was not afraid. I had a strange sense of
God's power flooding the inside of the twisted little car.

So powerful was it that I felt that the Lord was holding Gloria
to His chest — since I couldn't. He was taking her pain upon
Himself, as I would have done if I could. As I trembled, I felt the

literal presence of Jesus Christ. He was there. In the wrecked car beside us. I bowed myself to His authority. I thanked Him. I praised Him. I worshiped Him.

And as I held my hands steady to protect her head, I knew Jesus was comforting her, speaking to her unconscious mind, reassuring her gentle spirit.

Tenderly and compassionately, He spoke to my heart: "Take care of the natural. Don't worry. I will handle the supernatural."

I looked up.

And it was as if I saw the fury of the holy, mighty army of God. Angels of the Lord were engaged in battle against the forces of death and destruction. I rejoiced. There was no way the angel of death could get near our twisted little station wagon, for it was surrounded by great supernatural beings. And as I gazed out at this mighty display, I felt the Lord's voice. "Gloria belongs to Me. She is My daughter," He assured me. "She is dedicated to Me. I will protect her."

It was as if God was moving heaven and earth for this one dear woman. My spirit began to rejoice at the victory I was witnessing. "Thank you, Jesus," I murmured. I felt like a little child thanking my Daddy for the greatest gift ever given to me.

And in that moment, Gloria regained consciousness — although she was bleeding heavily internally and had bones broken in five places. She understood that I was there. As she slipped back out of awareness, I sensed her complete trust in the Lord. I was filled with a tremendous feeling of relief and gratitude.

One of the most beautiful things to see was the sincere concern of the people around me. A woman came forward and offered her business card. She had been a witness to the accident. She said that the truck had been at fault. She said she was willing to do anything to help us.

Then, the ambulance was there. And workers were moving the truck.

As our little station wagon shook and dropped to the ground, I felt the pain rip through Gloria. Yet, I also felt the presence of God all over the car. I felt that Gloria was surrounded by an invisible power force protecting her and watching over her as the twisted metal was removed.

The paramedics began to move her gently. Quickly they placed a brace on her neck, then put her on a stretcher. I had so many questions. I needed comfort.

"How is she going to be?" I asked.

Although the paramedic's answer was vague, I sensed a deep kindness. He truly understood how I felt. I was at peace. God had empowered me in a supernatural way. He had given me a glimpse of His power and His army.

In the next hours, I found myself in my office, where — alone — I released myself to the Lord. I cried and simply asked God to be in control. I could not be calm. I could not control the situation. Not without Him, anyway. I began to feel a serenity that cannot be described with words. I knew that Gloria was going to be fine. I believed and accepted that the Lord was with her.

Indeed, she had experienced a number of miracles — including a medically inexplicable halt in the internal bleeding while she was in the Emergency Room.

I began to understand the restlessness I had been feeling for two weeks. I had felt it as I delivered a message at an outreach conference. I had felt it when Gloria and I talked about a book I wanted to write — a spiritual warfare manual for believers. "Are you going to write about witchcraft again?" she had asked then. Then she had reminded me of my promise that I would not do a sequel to **Satan on the Loose,** *which had detailed my youth in rural Puerto Rico where I and my parents communed with evil spirits and practiced demonic healing and other witchcraft.*

"I'm not writing another book on witchcraft," I had assured her. "In this book, I want to warn of the forces that corrupt the Church and Christians." But I had understood her concern. While I was writing **Satan on the Loose,** *all hell had broken loose — literally. We had faced all types of demonic attack.*

I told Gloria that in this new book, I was firmly committed to exposing the devices of the enemy to undermine the Church. She had nodded silently. "Nicky," she had said, "I'm beginning to see you go through some changes. We cannot allow our family to go through what we went through last time."

"I understand," I had assured her. But I had been torn apart. In the next weeks, she and I would travel to England where we would see 12 straight days of power and glory as young people

packed auditoriums and gave their lives to Jesus. From there, without any rest, I would go to Poland.

There, one of the most magnificent things was to see Gloria's face light up with joy and love as thousands of people responded to the message. In Warsaw, 2,500 came to the Lord one night.

They had seen the movie, **The Cross and the Switchblade** *— in which actor Erik Estrada plays me and Pat Boone plays David Wilkerson. Polish versions of my book,* **Run, Baby, Run,** *had been widely distributed before the crusades.*

So, the people pressed forward, wanting to meet me, to shake my hand, to have me pray with them.

Several times, we'd almost been crushed *by the people pressing close. Gloria had been scared. Security guards escorted us out to safety, past clutching, reaching people with tears of joy on their faces. I was so moved during that tour of Poland. I sensed a great move of God's Spirit. For the first time, we were permitted to pass out literature and to put counseling material in the hands of those who streamed forward to the altar. It was a spiritual explosion. We saw 6,300 come to Jesus in those few days.*

"Gloria," I had said, "This is the place for you and I. These people are virgins in their hearts — they are not corrupted. They are not materialistic or hedonistic. They don't want to hear prosperity nor legalism. They are hungry and thirsty for God alone."

Gloria nodded in awe. Together, we pledged that upon our next visit, we would gain permission to bring in 75,000 Bibles.

Over the next months, that became my goal, *dream, prayer and desire. It turned into an intense passion, a drive compelling and consuming me.*

Yet, at the same time, we were having increasing confrontations with the satanists in Holland. In recent months they had become particularly bold — disrupting my crusades and flaunting their evil-glorifying worship of Lucifer.

Satan is misunderstood, they teach in dark sanctuaries filled with up to 500 nihilistic members. God isn't as good nor mighty as the Bible says — according to these angry, narcissistic, gratification-obsessed people, whose services are filled with sex, animal sacrifice, and unholy sacraments such as a profane anticommunion served before a reclining, nude woman.

Such seems impossible in America.

Yet, it is growing. I believe it is just one more sign that the end of time is upon us. These confused, power-hungry people are readying for the return of their great, evil messiah — the Antichrist.

The irony is so incredibly heart-breaking. I encountered them in Holland — a free, capitalistic, democratic, member of the western alliance and NATO — a country that evokes thoughts of windmills, tulips, wooden shoes and wholesome children ice-skating on picturesque canals. It's the land of Hans Brinker, Corrie ten Boom and good Queen Juliana. But in the company of Dutch satanists, one feels as if one has returned to Noah's day or Sodom and Gomorrah.

Yet, among the yearning Christians of Poland, I felt as if I were walking through the book of Acts. These people were committed to the death — standing up for Christ in a dark, communistic land filled with fear and death. They were experiencing God's mighty power. It had been wonderful for me to experience their joy with my beautiful Gloria at my side.

***Gloria* ....**

When I arrived back at the hospital, she urged me to catch a plane and go ahead to my scheduled, two-day speaking engagement. "Go for it!" she enthused from her bed in the intensive care unit. "Go on! Conquer!"

So, I went.

As I arrived at Denver's airport, I went to wait for my connecting flight. There, a minister recognized me. He grabbed my hand and began to pray for me and Gloria. He encouraged me. He asked the Lord to surround me with serenity.

I suspect that we may have looked like a couple of fools right there in the middle of the waiting area, but that man just raised his heart to heaven.

I don't even know his name. He said the Lord had guided him to be there to meet me and pray for me.

He had not heard anything about Gloria's accident yet.

But as I told him a little of what had happened, I secretly thanked God for having someone waiting there with a message of hope. It had been no coincidence.

Then, on the plane, the evil darkness made one last attempt. I found myself sitting next to a professing witch — which, as you know, has happened before.

But this time, I was filled with greater boldness.

"You can't touch me," I spoke to the evil one within her. "I belong to Jesus."

The woman sneered.

But she left me alone in my thoughts.

Six days after the accident, Gloria was released from the hospital. Today she remembers little of the wreck, except that I was there with her — somehow. But she is quick to give the praise and glory to Jesus. He delivered her from what appeared to be certain death.

By the time she had arrived at the hospital, there was no sign of any glass cuts on her face, although it was covered with blood. Jesus had taken her pain and her fear.

There was little that remained as evidence of her escape from death. But I was there. And I remember.

I remember the presence of the Lord — and how He always comes through.

I remember the angels.

I remember the peace.

And I remember the victory.

The victory is ours!

In front of me, the television is blaring. A news anchorman is quizzing an evangelist who is telling how he knew long ago all about the deep evil in another recently disgraced evangelist's life. The speaker holds up a tape cassette, which he says, proves his allegations.

The newsman asks him to play it for listeners to hear. The guest stalls, momentarily at a loss for words. His eyes dart and he smiles as another guest interrupts — diverting attention onto another accusation. I suspect that the tape is *Greatest Country Hits* or *How to Buy Real Estate With No Money Down* and that my colleague in the spreading of the Gospel — this fellow evangelist holding up his cassette — is a liar.

But the damage is done.

One more man of God is discredited before all who have tuned in to witness the latest skirmish in our darkening Holy Wars.

"No," my soul cries. "No more."

How did our Church get to this terrible place in history?

Well, it was foretold in Scripture:

"I know you well," reads the book of Revelation —

"— you are neither hot nor cold. ... You say, 'I am rich, with everything I want; I don't need a thing!' And you don't realize that spiritually you are wretched and miserable and poor and blind and naked" (Rev. 3:15-19).

My eyes glance over to my coffee table. There, another highly respected evangelist's face smiles out from a slick, full-color letter. Screaming headlines and stamped messages all over the envelope proclaim that God has a magnificent miracle waiting for me. All I have to do is take four envelopes and write four key words on them. Then, I need to write four checks and put them in the envelopes and send them to the ministry over the next four weeks.

After I have done so, the letter testifies, God will give me the miracle of my choice.

My heart cries out at this terrible prostitution of the Gospel. And as I gaze up at the sputtering fraud on TV, I know how we got ourselves into this terrible fix.

Because we would not clean our own house.

We would not follow the biblical guidelines for calling erring brothers and sisters to task. Instead, we waited until the sin was so evil that God let Babylon do our job.

Just that evening, I had watched parts of three Christian broadcasts. Two concentrated heavily on the urgent need for more money to continue their ministries.

The teaching centered on how the listener would be blessed by God if he or she obeyed the commandments about tithing, generosity and spreading the Gospel.

The evangelist and his wife read letter after letter from people upset because this particular show had been taken off of some local stations. The evangelist could not pay his bills. The message was clear and urgent: Send money! Keep us on the air to help these poor, hurting people!

I noticed that the evangelist read only letters lifting him up. Seemingly each writer had nothing but praise for the evangelist. Each went into great detail as to how his message of faith and hope and power had changed the writer's life. The evangelist seemed to be telling his viewers: *I'm doing my job, so why aren't you doing yours by sending me the money I need? Hurry! I'm facing deadlines!*

A half-hour later, another evangelist's son wept about how misunderstood his father was — and began itemizing all the wonderful things their ministry had done. The message again: *Send more money quickly.* On and on the young man went, telling about this outreach and that crusade, this life changed and that marriage restored.

"God needs you to pick up your phone and call in your pledge," the young man repeated. "He can't write out a check. But you can."

I winced in pain. Of course God can write a check — or at least cause it to be written. He could touch my heart and convict me to send a check. This young man was praying to the wrong person. He was asking **me** to provide.

He would do a lot better to be asking God.

I would obey the Lord telling me to write him a check. I trust my heavenly Father. But my spirit will allow me to trust this young heir.

Now, I stand up and walk across the room as the newscaster talks with a former employee of a large ministry. New details of lust and greed fill the airwaves.

Saddened, I find myself fumbling in my Bible for the eleventh chapter of the Apostle Paul's second letter to the church in Corinth. Paul's heart, too, was broken! Just listen to him as he sorts through his thoughts:

"I hope you will be patient with me as I keep on talking like a fool. Do bear with me and let me say what is on my heart. I am anxious for you — with the deep concern of God himself —" (verses 1 and 2).

Friend, I pray you will *feel* Paul's hurt as he writes these next thoughts, paraphrased from Paul's original Greek words by Bible scholar Kenneth Taylor in *The Living Bible:*

*"But I am frightened, fearing that in some way you will be led away from your pure and simple devotion to our Lord, just as Eve was deceived by Satan in the Garden of Eden. **You seem so gullible: you believe whatever anyone tells you,** even if he is preaching about another Jesus than the one we preach ...*

"You swallow it all.

*"Did I do wrong and cheapen myself and make you look down on me because I preached God's Good News to you without charging you anything? **I have never yet asked you for one cent, and I never will!***

***"God never sent those men at all; they are 'phonies' who have fooled you into thinking they are Christ's apostles.** Yet I am not surprised! Satan can change himself into an angel of light, so it is no wonder his servants can do it too, and seem like godly ministers"* (II Cor. 11:3-15).

Read what Peter told the church in II Peter 2:3:

"These teachers in their greed will tell you anything to get hold of your money. But God condemned them long ago and their destruction is on the way."

Listen to Jude writing in verse 8 of his epistle:

"These false teachers carelessly go right on living their evil, immoral lives, degrading their bodies and laughing at those in authority over them ...."

The hour is late.
I turn off the TV. Paul's words to the Galatians ring in my ears:

"I am amazed that you are turning away so soon from God who, in his love and mercy, invited you to share in the eternal life he gives through Christ; you are already following a different 'way to heaven,' which really doesn't go to heaven at all. For there is no other way ..." (Gal. 1:6,7)

And I fall on my face before the Lord God. Forgive us, Father. We have become moneychangers in Your temple, manipulating God's people with lies and deceptions to get them to send us Your tithes and offerings.

We have become Christian humanists — weeping on the television that listeners must help You out by sending their money so that poor Almighty God can continue His work. We have turned our backs on humility to become braggarts as we build up our ministries so people will continue to support us ...

My beautiful wife, Gloria, is reading over my shoulder now as I write these thoughts.

"Nicky, Nicky," she cautions, "Why are you so angry? Don't be so harsh! Where is your love? Don't discourage people with how bad things are. Show them the hope of Jesus."

She's right.

Absolutely!

Forgive me, brothers and sisters!

I believe you needed to hear these words of warning. However, it would be so wrong if all I managed to do was discourage you.

We will win this battle!

"With God before us," proclaimed Paul, writing to the church in Rome, "who can come against us?"

"O Jacob, O Israel," cried the Prophet Isaiah —

"how can you say that the Lord doesn't see your troubles and isn't being fair? Don't you yet understand? Don't you know by now that the everlasting God, the Creator of the farthest parts of the earth, never grows faint or weary? No one can fathom the depths of his understanding. He gives power to the tired and worn out, and strength to the weak. Even the youths shall be exhausted, and the young men will all give up. But they that wait upon the Lord shall renew their strength. They shall mount up with wings like eagles; they shall run and not be weary; they shall walk and not faint" (Isaiah 40:27-31).

How will this happen?

"If my people will humble themselves and pray, and search for me, and turn from their wicked ways, I will hear them from heaven and forgive their sins and heal their land" (II Chron. 7:14).

I reach up and touch Gloria's hand.

I praise God that God gave me such a wonderful spouse, best friend and advisor.

Through her, He has taught me so much and shown me His truths.

Such as that Satan's evil does not have to touch us.

And that we are conquerors.

Brothers and sisters, we have a problem. We have forgotten Who is God. We have twisted such scriptures as Psalm 82:6 and John 10:34. We think we are God.

We are not.

This problem has brought some of our Lord's greatest servants down in humiliation and shame. Our natural lust for money, fame, applause, power and acclaim is not His plan for us.

We have violated God's laws.

We need to reexamine the faith of our forefathers.

We need to humble ourselves in brokenness, willing to sacrifice all.

We must admit that God is the only god and we are not. We do not make the rules.

He does. He has told us what we are supposed to be doing — seeking His holiness, praising His name ... winning the lost.

We are His most perfect creation, the one being made in His likeness. We are His delight. We are meant to spend eternity with Him.

The deceiver has tried to rob Him of us. Satan wants us to inflict on us the terrible eternity that awaits him.

Let's get about God's business and quit falling for Satan's traps. After all, we have the key to terrorize hell! Falling on our faces before our Lord, let's renew our fear of our loving God. We must seek His ways for us, too.

We might lose some battles, but that's not so bad if we are forced to learn to depend on Jesus Christ!

We must listen to His voice.

We must quit bickering over foolish human dogma. We must spurn the Christian superstar mentality. We must go back to Pentecost — paying careful attention on what to expect.

Yes, we will have some Ananiases and Sapphiras, struck down in our midst as they attempt to deceive not only God's people, but also the Holy Spirit.

There will be more Simon the Sorcerers — trying to buy God's power for their own selfish purposes.

And, sadly, there will be Stephens, too — killed by the forces of evil, but raised to victory in glory.

But there will also be Barnabases — simple men given tasks such as to go out and testify to men who have sworn to murder them — such as Saul of Tarsus.

There will be Pauls. Because of Barnabas' faithful, unafraid obedience, Saul was transformed into Paul the Apostle, the greatest Christian missionary and writer of the Epistles.

And, praise God, there will be Timothies — young men and women full of faith and power, ready to take the Good News into the next generation.

Brothers and sisters, we have a problem. But we are going to survive this dark hour. We are stronger now.

We have learned some hard lessons.

But we are not defeated.

We are destined to **win.**

**Would you like to know
more about Nicky's ministry?**

Write to him at:

Nicky Cruz Outreach
P.O. Box 25070
Colorado Springs, Colorado 80936